MADHAV RAO SCINDIA OF GWALIOR 1876-1925

MADHAV RAO SCINDIA OF GWALIOR 1876-1925

H. M. BULL

GYAN

Published by

Gyan Publishing House
5, Ansari Road
Daryaganj, New Delhi-110002
Phone: 011-47034999, 9811692060
E-mail: books@gyanbooks.com

Distribution Network
gyanbooks.com
India, USA, Canada, UK, Australia

ISBN: 978-93-7225-804-2 (PB)

First Published, 1926

2nd Impression 2026

Printed at: Gyan Press, Delhi.

MADHAV RAO SCINDIA OF GWALIOR 1876-1925
Author: H. M. BULL

MADHAV RAO SCINDIA

OF

GWALIOR.

1876–1925

"Princes are like to heavenly bodies, which cause good or evil times, and which have much veneration, but no rest."

—*BACON.*

H. M. Bull.

K. N. Haksar.

PREFACE.

For practical purposes this memoir may be said to have been finished over a year ago, when, in its manuscript form, it was laid aside by its joint authors to whom its complete inadequacy was, and still is, apparent.

They did not anticipate that any sudden inspiration would visit them, but they recognised the possibility of a record, more worthy of the subject, being compiled by some abler pen than their own.

That possibility remaining still unrealised, these pages now attain to the dignity of print thanks to the munificence of Sardar M. N. Sitole, nephew of the late Maharaja and premier noble of the Gwalior State.

The writers of this book herewith acknowledge their gratitude to the Governor of a Province for his most valuable criticisms and further admit their heavy debt to a prominent Indian Civilian who laboriously waded through a faulty typescript line by line and valiantly strove to purge the text of its grossest errors of style. It is only their expressed wish for anonymity which prevents these two friends of Madhav Rao Scindia from being mentioned here by name.

Mr. Y. T. Mangaokar, the Manager of the Alijah Darbar Press, Gwalior, has taken great pains with the production of this volume, and to his expert assiduity must be ascribed any merit in its appearance.

GWALIOR :
October, 1926.

H. M. B.
K. N. H.

CONTENTS.

PORTRAITS

OF

MADHAV RAO SCINDIA.

MADHAV RAO SCINDIA OF GWALIOR,

1876–1925.

CHAPTER I.

THE STAGE AND A PROLOGUE.

A land where throughout the summer months even the night but seldom brings relief after the weary hours of daylight, while from early morn the heavy dust haze serves but to blunt the edges of the shimmering horizon yet is powerless to temper the molten heat that streams down from a cloudless sky above and beats up from the parched and cracking ground underfoot, a land where from the arrival of the monsoon (though every three or four years the gods forget to send the rains) the thunder-laden atmosphere reeks with fever and is ever from sundown vocal "with the moan of insects seeking blood;" yet a land too where, for the fleeting space of the four cold weather months, the climate rivals that of the Riviera, and the dry clean air, for all that the sea is hundreds of miles away, builds up the health of a sturdy peasantry and induces a momentary forgetfulness of the ordeal by fire that from April to July is the annual penance of those cultivators and their cattle. Such a land is Northern Gwalior.

But Malwa, Scindia's fat province to the south, is almost a different world. Secure from scorching heats and biting cold, Malwa, perhaps of all parts of India, most nearly approaches the ideal of a land where it is always afternoon. Its inhabitants are not tried during May and June in a fiery furnace, but they miss too the bracing breath of winter. Those summer nights of Malwa when the stars—was it this that moved old Raja Jai Singh to build an observatory at Ujjain?—burn clear and big in a pellucid sky which never entirely loses its tint of turquoise, those nights, the "Shab-i-Malwa," have grown into an Indian proverb expressive of nocturnal bliss.

The easy-going folk of the Malwa plateau know not the terrors of the dread *loo,* that hot wind which for days on end drives unceasingly across the superheated plain that stretches north and east of the historic Rock of Gwalior. The children of Ujjain, that ancient city, more ancient in the local estimation than Benares and possibly no less sacred, do not like those of Lashkar, the modern capital of Scindia's realm, run to their parents in summer-time with cries of "my head, my head" nor, like the Shunammite's son, wilt away stricken by the sun or its engendered heat.

Compared with the other tracts of the Gwalior State, Malwa in several ways enjoys an ampler meed of blessing. With its renowned black cotton soil, this province, the first of Scindia's conquests, is practically immune from famine. Unlike the cultivator of the light sands and loams of the Northern districts, the Malwa peasant in years of scanty rainfall is not forced to migrate with his cattle in a desperate adventure to keep his plough oxen or milch buffaloes alive until the break of the next monsoon.

Here on the tableland they need not those protective works of irrigation which are essential to the security of the monotonous plain that starting from Lashkar crumbles at last into the ravines of the Chambal, the river that since 1804 has formed the boundary of the northernmost tract still under the rule of any Maratha prince.

In times of pinching scarcity, Malwa is an habitual refuge not only for the foodless folk of Northern Gwalior, but also for huge droves of kine which straggle southwards in charge of gaunt, wild-looking herdsmen from the wastes of Rajputana. The passage of these nomad strangers, often on the verge of starvation, presents a serious problem to the authorities of the districts through which they wander.

With an area of something over 25,000 square miles the Gwalior State—it is much about the size of Scotland—is far from being a compact dominion. The northern block, embracing roughly two-thirds of the whole, is indeed united and forms a geographical entity. But the southern tracts comprise four main, yet separate districts, no single *Zila* of those *Zilas* (to use the local name) abutting on the main block or on another.

Apart from these, especially in the south and west of the State, there are a number of isolated patches of territory, none of any great size, some indeed solitary island villages, but all alike hemmed in by the lands of other principalities in Central India, while lastly may be mentioned a few survivals of a lordship once exercised over a large part of Rajasthan by the famous Mahadji Scindia, stray remnants of past conquests, to-day completely enringed by some Rajput dominion.

The scattered nature of these territories renders administration neither cheap nor easy; rather it occasions continual boundary disputes and frequent requests for the extradition of offenders against law. Admittedly these remote corners of Scindia's domain do now and again harbour more than a few dacoits and other desperadoes; but at least the density of their population, as compared with that of the neighbouring States, would seem to indicate that their inhabitants find little real fault with the Gwalior laws under which they dwell.

The Vindhya hills form a watershed in which practically all the rivers of Gwalior have their source and thence flow north or south. Whatever be the scenery through which they run, these streams as streams suffer from a depressing seasonal monotony. During the rainy months they swell into raging torrents which bear away precious silt to fatten other lands, and especially Bengal; their turbid rush makes communications difficult and often works much damage. But, once the last monsoon shower has fallen, their flow soon degenerates into a mere trickle or ceases entirely, and leaves a glaring sandy bed varied occasionally by outcrops of bare rock which in places may hold up large pools of water, the haunt of the wary crocodile.

No river of Gwalior is navigable, none serviceable even for floating down forest produce during the spasm of its flooding. For irrigation purposes too most of these streams are useless, so deep is the channel they have fretted for themselves between their high banks of sand or rock.

Much of the State, more particularly in its northern section, is too stony or too shallow-soiled to repay regular cultivation. Such barren expanses are in many places covered with thorny scrub jungle in which tigers abound; but such "forests" have few big trees, and afford little or no heavy timber for commercial use. Firewood and charcoal they supply in plenty as well as an abundance of rough grass; but to retain its fodder value, this grass needs cutting just before its seed falls in October or November, months when the rush of agricultural operations and the seasonal prevalence of malaria prohibit any large supply of casual labour.

No longer in the Gwalior jungles are to be found the herds of wild elephants which once gave sport to the Moghul Emperors in their progresses to and from the Deccan. The massive boles against which the great beasts tried their tusks have been long ago cut down, felled partly for timber, partly to provide fuel for iron smelters. In the past, at least, no attempt was made to replace the fallen giants, and despite measures of afforestation in recent years, the State can anticipate little direct return from its woodlands for several decades to come.

Nor again is Gwalior blessed by rich deposits of metals or minerals. Iron ore abounds, but of coal there is none and of manganese none of commercial worth. While the stone quarries are admittedly valuable the cost of transportation as a rule precludes any but the local utilisation of the material extracted. The sand and lime stones of the north serve admirably for building purposes, and the roofing slabs and beams hewn from them are of exceptional length and strength.

In Malwa the rocks are mainly Deccan Trap, a black stone of adamantine hardness. So difficult is it to handle that it is seldom brought into common use save as foundations for houses, a wooden frame work being erected on squared basalt blocks, and the space between the timber uprights filled in with brick. No longer is Malwa "a land where human labour and life are cheaper than bread." The cost of basalt ashlars so commonly utilised in the past for temple walls or the palaces of grandees in Avantika, is to-day prohibitive even for the dwellings of the wealthiest merchants in that province. It is otherwise with the more tractable sandstone, and houses with walls, beams, and roofs of this material, so frequently to be seen in Lashkar, are by common consent better for health and comfort than the more picturesque dwellings of brick and timber in Ujjain, for all the attraction of their red-tiled roofs.

As yet Scindia's dominions show little sign of modern industrialisation. Save for a number of cotton gins, more cotton presses than are justified by the present demand, and a few spinning and weaving mills, Gwalior can boast of hardly a single factory worked by power.

The main occupation of its people is agriculture, and this directly supports the bulk of the three and a quarter million subjects of Scindia. Even in the so-called towns, other than Lashkar, the present capital, and Ujjain, which till 1810 held that position, a large proportion of the inhabitants employ themselves chiefly in tillage of the soil. Such centres of population are but overgrown villages, in which the inhabitants retain their rural character, careless of higher things. Not many years ago an Inspector-General of Municipalities in the State, having refused the request of one such overgrown village for a town-committee on the plea that the place was devoid of any signs of town-life, was naively requested to explain where "urban characteristics" were obtainable and to state the price of such amenities ! Did the State Workshops supply them ?

The light soils of the great alluvial plain lying north and east of Lashkar possesses but moderate fertility, and artificial irrigation, still chiefly supplied from wells by bullock power, is a necessity for securing a good harvest.

In this matter of soil as in other things, Malwa differs widely from the rest of the State. On this plateau—it averages some 1,600 feet above sea-level—two crops, the autumn or *Kharif* and the spring or *Rabi*, are raised as on the northern plains, but here artificial watering can be dispensed with except for sugarcane and the more delicate poppy, the latter, since the prohibition of opium export to China, covering but a fraction of its acreage sown some twenty years ago.

On plain or plateau alike the Gwalior peasant is usually a man who farms but a few acres of unfenced ground which he rents from the *Zamindar* or State-appointed landlord of his village. The smallness of the holdings and the lack of combination among the cultivators preclude the general use of modern agricultural machinery no less than the adoption of scientific methods of tillage. Though there is a marked difference, mental as well as physical, between the peasantry of the plateau and that of the plain, and though they speak distinct dialects, yet both in like degree display an innate suspicion of innovation, preferring those usages of sowing, cultivation, and harvest commonly practised since their forbears tilled the lands of Lord Vikramaditya of Ujjain, India's counterpart to King Arthur of Britain.

None the less, for all their primitive methods, the peasants of Gwalior are, in fact, as the late Maharaja Madhav Rao Scindia, so often called them the "Anna-Data" or the bread givers and so the mainstay of the State. In normal years they produce a large surplus of wheat, cotton, and oil-seeds for export to British India and the great world beyond.

A purely agricultural country, handicapped by antiquated modes of husbandry, Gwalior still could support a far larger population than it does to-day. Indeed in the past, if credence be given to that Moghul Domesday Book, the Ain-i-Akbari, the provinces which are now comprised in Scindia's dominions were, to judge from the revenue demanded and collected three centuries ago, far more densely peopled then than is the case to-day.

For this decrease of the folk the reasons are various but indisputable. As the rivers gnaw deeper and deeper into the sandy soils of Northern Gwalior, the water level in the wells is steadily sinking. Possibly the extensive denudation of the forests has reduced the annual rainfall since the spacious days of Akbar. There can, however, be no doubt that during the decay of the Moghul Empire, life and property were rendered insecure and especially so for the ryot who from time immemorial had passed his days toiling in the fields. Hitherto practically untouched by internecine, dynastic, or religious wars, the peasantry was looted each year by marauding bands of Marathas from the Deccan. To crown all, in the early part of the nineteenth century, the State bore the brunt of the Pindari ravages. These intermittent calamities have admittedly contributed to reduce the population of the provinces that to-day own the sway of Scindia as their lord and master.

The Scindias who to-day control the destinies of the Gwalior State are sprung from a stock which forms one of the ninety-six *kulas* or clans under which are grouped all pure-bred Marathas. Hence in name at least Gwalior is a Maratha State ; in name rather than in reality, for, though the term be used with full elasticity, there are in all barely sixteen thousand men, women, and children of Maratha parentage among the three and a quarter million persons over whose lives Scindia's will is absolute.

The ruling family and the chief Sardars (nobles) of the State are Marathas, and claim to be of original Rajput stock, either descendants of *Kshatriya* families who retired before successive waves of iconoclastic Islam or cadets of such houses who, centuries ago, adventurously left their desert homes to carve out estates and careers for themselves in the Deccan.

But even if, unlike the law courts in the recent Tanjore succession case, the Rajputs of Gwalior admit the Marathas' claim to Kshatriya birth, they, until recent years, regarded their conquerors as upstarts. Any undignified action on the part of the rulers would be explained and reprobated in the sarcastic phrase "*Maratha Darbar hai*," it is a Maratha Government. So what better can be expected ?

It is exactly two centuries ago this year (1926) since the founder of the Scindia dynasty received from the Peshwa his first commission to collect in northern Malwa the *Chauth* (25 per cent of the revenue) and the *Sardeshmukhi* (an additional 10 per cent) and was allowed to retain half the *Mokassa* or balance for the remuneration of himself and his horsemen. It was practically fifty years later ere the great Mahadji Scindia dared administer a slice of Malwa as his own domain and not as a fief held from his overlord at Poona.

In India where, if life is short, memory at least is long, two hundred years is no great space in which a subjugated population, kept in check for most of the time by fear rather than by affection, can be expected to forget the real or tinsel glories of an imagined golden past. Religious etiquette perhaps even more than religious sentiment, may prescribe for the Hindu a blind acceptance of the master whom fate has set over him, but such a potentate, though admittedly a Hindu, if an alien by caste or custom, is only tolerated and not loyally served, unless by his acts he can fire the imagination of his subjects and guided by a happy star, recall the exploits of some mythical hero-king of pre-historic times.

That in this respect at least Madhav Rao Scindia was fortunate, and that he roused in his subjects' hearts a loyalty based on a personal devotion, is a claim which, it is thought, the following pages will be found to substantiate.

This no place to narrate at length the history of the Scindia dynasty from its first obscure origins, nor to tell of Ranoji, a poor relation of a family which held the position of *Patel* or headman in the village of Kanarkhera, some sixteen miles east of Satara. Suffice it to say that, though poverty had forced Ranoji to become the personal attendant of the Peshwa Balaji Baji Rao, his talents lifted him from the humble post of slipper bearer to that of a famous leader of irregular horse and the collector of revenue for the province of Malwa, where in 1745 he died at Shujalpur.

It is unnecessary to devote space to his immediate successors his two sons, Jayappa and Dattaji, both rather shadowy figures, or to his grandson, the luckless

Jankuji, a mere boy who after his capture at the battle of Panipat in 1761 was executed in cold blood by his conqueror, Ahmad Shah Abdali.

So too we must resist the temptation to dwell on the career of the next Scindia, Mahadji, Ranoji's natural son, whose proved ability enabled him to rise superior to the accident of his birth. It is enough to state that aided by the loyal services of Benoit de Boigne, the greatest of the many military adventurers in Hindustan, this Prince by his innate sagacity and political acumen, left at his death in 1794 a dominion which stretched from beyond Delhi in the north to the Nerbudda and yet further south of that river. Though in name a servant of the Moghul Emperor on the one hand and a vassal of the Peshwa on the other, he held the reality of power over most of Hindustan west of the river Jumna as well as in the most fertile tracts of Rajputana.

The follies and failures of Daulat Rao, Mahadji's successor by adoption, might attract the moralist, but to the historian of the House of Gwalior they form a sorry tale. Of tender age at his accession, within the space of ten years Daulat Rao after a war against the British had lost all his territories north of the river Chambal and south of the Ajanta hills. Although, by the "mulk-giri" or land grabbing expeditions of his Italian General Jean Baptiste Filose, he was able to filch certain districts from his weaker Rajput neighbours, and thus in some measure to counterbalance his losses round Agra, Delhi, and Aligarh, his rule was conspicuous for no single action designed to promote the good of his State.

His great-grandson, Madhav Rao Scindia, once commented after his perusal of "Wheeler's Summary of Maratha Affairs"—

> "For his house had Mahadji won a crown;
> From Daulat Rao's head it toppled down."

Yet in spite of the territory he had lost, Daulat Rao was treated by the East India Company as an independent potentate occupying a position which differed much from that of those Chiefs on whom a subsidiary force had been imposed. A picturesque, but veracious chronicle of those times, "Letters from a Maratha Camp," gives interesting details of the respect accorded to Daulat Rao by the servants of John Company. It also portrays this particular Scindia as possessing no qualities of military leadership and fewer still of administrative genius. The book presents a vivid description of Court intrigues, mutinous soldiery, and an utter disregard of the sufferings of the civil population in those tracts of Rajputana through which for years Scindia's army marched up and down collecting tribute.

If bygones are to be bygones and Maratha and Rajput are in future to dwell in peace and amity together, Madhav Rao Scindia was indubitably correct in his dictum that these Letters, which have no claim to literary merit, were hardly suitable for adoption as a textbook at the Mayo College, Ajmere. The members of the Managing Committee of Chiefs' Colleges, however, have no voice in matters of curriculum, and for several years the Letters remained in the English course.

In 1827 Daulat Rao Scindia died. In his latter years his relations with the British had grown more amicable than they had been during the first two decades of his rule. To the end he had always looked on the Deccan (thither on his death-bed his face was turned) as his home and, though childless, had refused to nominate a successor.

Jankoji Rao who followed by adoption was a boy of eleven whom Daulat Rao's widow, Baiza Bai, purposely kept without education. The child grew up completely at the mercy of his adoptive mother's whims and tempers and totally unable to control his turbulent troops or to check the feuds and intrigues of his nobles. Until after countless plots and quarrels Baiza Bai was finally expelled from the State, this lady did much to debase the fortunes of Gwalior by her ceaseless attempts to further her own ends and those of her favourites. Jankoji Rao, for all his loyalty to his allies, the British, and his impeccable intentions, was incapable of filling the position of an autocratic ruler. The deplorable state of his Court, the absence of any real administration, and the indifference of the chief to the sufferings of his *ryots* have found an eloquent historian in Colonel Sleeman who later became the Resident at Gwalior.

Early in 1843 Jankoji Rao died, childless as his two predecessors had been. Though nominally as independent a ruler as Daulat Rao, his lack of capacity had made various encroachments on his powers on easy matter for the Residency whither as a child he had twice fled for refuge from his adoptive mother's tantrums. The selection by his thirteen-year-old widow of a boy of eight who succeeded as Jayaji Rao could not fail to facilitate this process.

The first year following this child's accession saw Gwalior rent by internal feuds and at the mercy of the undisciplined mob into which the battalions, once de Boigne's pride, had already degenerated. Intrigues at the Court and the unscrupulous action of Dada Khasgiwala, the Comptroller of the Household, culminated in the intervention of Lord Ellenborough, the Governor-General, who in person, marched into Gwalior with an army. The two battles of Maharajpur and Panniar were fought, both on the same day, and the State lay at the mercy of the British.

No overt attempt was made to lower the status of Scindia's dominion, but a considerable slice of its territory was assigned for the support of a largely increased Contingent Force, while at the same time the strength of the Gwalior Army was materially reduced. This reduction was most salutary: for years Lashkar had been at the mercy of a rabble of soldiery, and a large decline in the revenues of the State had made their regular payment difficult. That the increase of the Gwalior Contingent, a body of soldiers dating from the days of Doulat Rao's time and re-organised in those of Jankoji Rao, was a mistake, in spite of these troops being officered by a British Staff, the English were soon to learn in the days of the Mutiny.

Lord Ellenborough was satisfied with his work, even if the British Parliament was with difficulty convinced that the action taken had been justified. After setting up the first Council of Regency that Gwalior had ever seen, the Governor-General withdrew, secure in the knowledge that the Council would act on the advice of the Resident. Automatically, it was believed, Scindia's position would come to approximate to that of less prominent States.

The next decade witnessed unusual progress. In 1853 the young Maharaja received his powers and, thanks to the ability of the Brahman Dinkar Rao whose capacity had shortly before secured his promotion to the post of *Diwan*, Gwalior made rapid strides. Reforms were introduced into many branches of the administration, and lawlessness was sternly suppressed.

A year later Major Charters Macpherson became the Resident at Gwalior, and rapidly establishing the most cordial relations with the young Prince, he persuaded Jayaji Rao to pay a visit to Calcutta early in 1857. Dinkar Rao too was of the party, and the *Diwan's* ability and sincerity made a great impression on those Members of the Governor-General's Council with whom he came in contact.

Little more than two months after the Maharaja's return to his home, the terror of the Mutiny flared up, and Gwalior in an instant reverted to the conditions which had prevailed in 1843.

The Gwalior Contingent at Morar rose and killed its English Officers, the State troops at Lashkar became openly disloyal, and the general feeling at Scindia's Court was strongly anti-British. For all this, Jayaji Rao remained absolutely staunch. By a variety of pretexts he confined his mutinous soldiery within the limits of his territories. For a twelvemonth the State troops were kept inactive, ever restrained by the expectation that on the morrow they would be led to swell the main body of mutineers.

From Agra whither he had been forced to flee, Major Macpherson kept up daily communication with the Maharaja and his Chief Minister. Scindia still held his troops in idleness until, at last, towards the end of May, 1858, Tantia Topi and Lachmi Bai, "The Rani of Continsi" approached Lashkar and summoned Scindia to the Gwalfim.

A picturesque, but untrue, story relates that the Maharaja himself replied by firing a cannon into Tantia Topi's camp. It goes on to say that the Rani herself charged the Gwalior Artillery, cut down the gunners, and after routing the army, spared Jayaji Rao's life as that of a "misguided youth."

The less romantic truth is that the Maharaja led out his troops to give battle to the mutineers only to see his army desert *en masse* to the enemy. With his Maratha body-guard which alone remained staunch, Jayaji Rao fled with Dinkar Rao to Agra. Behind him Tantia Topi was looting his capital.

Though in his anxiety at the time he could not possibly have recognised the fact, the Maharaja might justly have asserted the claim, since admitted by posterity, that he had achieved "a political triumph without which India could hardly have been saved."

CHAPTER II.

THE PROLOGUE CONCLUDED. MORE STAGE SETTING.

IN perusing the chronicles of the Indian States during the past century, indeed in watching their political life to-day, a common phenomenon observable is that of the sudden dismissal or the forced resignation of some minister whose integrity and ability have been in striking contrast to the dishonesty and mediocrity of his fellow officials. Occasionally, and then perhaps the metal is but silver-gilt, he may be found left in possession of his high office and its emoluments, but shorn of all power for enlightened reform, and reduced in an instant to an administrative nonentity.

Of such catastrophes members of the Political Department of the Government of India have frequently been the unconscious agents. In these Principalities where to this day the administration remains really personal notwithstanding make-believe constitutions, they have time and again found one man, the *Diwan* of the State to which they were accredited or some other high official, who was obviously a person of outstanding merit and capacity as well as genuinely eager to forward the best interests of his Prince's dominions. Sincerely attracted by such a personality, the Resident or Political

Agent has perhaps made the easy mistake of considering the minister as greater, not merely as more capable, than the master.

Secure in the knowledge that the real sovereignty in India abides in the British Government whose servant he is, the political officer in his anxiety to further progress disregards the fact that the pinchbeck imitation of sovereignty, or, if the word "sovereignty" be held objectionable, the power claimed by the titular and autocratic head of a Native State, is an actuality, based not merely on the fond belief of the Ruler himself, but also on the deep-rooted sentiment of that Ruler's subjects.

The result is always the same, always equally distressing. As already stated, the minister is dismissed, or else forced to resign, or if he remains in office, becomes a mere figure-head, powerless for good or evil, but in any case suspect.

Dinkar Rao's sagacity had been of immense worth to Maharaja Jayaji Rao during the terror of the Mutiny, but, for all the support he derived from his *Diwan*, that Prince's native wit, to assess his loyalty at its lowest value (and he was loyal not merely from enlightened self-interest) would have kept him to the last true to his treaty obligations with the British.

Despite his youth, Jayaji Rao was the shrewdest Maratha Chief of his day, indeed was probably the shrewdest pure-bred Maratha then alive in Gwalior. The effective subterfuges which he had employed to keep his rebel army actively idle—and the times demanded subterfuge rather than diplomacy—were the product of his subtle brain and not the invention of any adviser.

For a bare three weeks Jayaji Rao remained at Agra, an exile from his State and capital. Then he returned to Lashkar to be re-instated by Sir Hugh Rose who had routed the mutineers and occupied the fortress of Gwalior.

With the Maharaja returned the minister, Dinkar Rao, to begin the task of putting right the disorder left by Tantia Topi's occupation and pillage of the capital. Back too came Major Macpherson, the Resident, in ill health and worn out by the strain of the preceding twelvemonth.

The mutineers had been scattered; "The Rani of Jhansi" had been cut down by a trooper in an engagement not half a mile from the site now occupied by the massive Jai Bilas Palace; Tantia Topi was a fugitive, shortly to be surrendered and hanged at Sipri, a town some seventy miles south-west of Lashkar. Jayaji Rao, always generous in individual cases, was already contemplating the gift of estates to his Brahmin minister and to certain Maratha Sardars who had loyally stood by him in his extremity and shared his flight to Agra.

Yet Dinkar Rao had many enemies who were not likely to forgive the humiliation of their defeat. Perhaps to them may be traced the first whisper that the *Diwan* was already being treated by the British Government as a person of practically the same importance as his lord and master. May be the minister was too prone to play in Gwalior the *rôle* of Cicero and to voice some vernacular variant of the Roman's wearisome refrain, "*O fortunatam natam, me consule, Romam.*"

Dinkar Rao's elevation to the post of *Diwan* had been the work of the British Government: it had never been popular with the big Maratha Sardars. While so conspicuous a personality held the position of chief minister, what hope had they of attaining to such an office with its multifold opportunities for fostering their own private interests or for furthering their personal vendettas?

A rumour, soon to prove well founded, spread at Lashkar. Dinkar Rao was losing the Maharaja's confidence, though it was still less than a year since Jayaji Rao's triumphal return to his capital. Once before in 1854, between the departure of one Political Agent and the arrival of another, Dinkar Rao had been deprived of power. Could not his complete overthrow be now engineered?

In 1859 Macpherson relinquished charge of the Gwalior Residency, and his successor had on several occasions to intervene in the settlement of misunderstandings between Jayaji Rao and his minister.

For all his efforts, their relations grew daily worse, and the Maharaja in high dudgeon withdrew to Sipri. He is reported to have said "Either I or Dinkar Rao will rule in Gwalior."

With all speed the *Diwan* followed his master and, being granted an interview, tendered the resignation of his high office. He retired to Allahabad with the intention of passing a life of meditation on the banks of the holy Ganges. Fate, however, had destined that his work as a statesman was not yet to end.

As a Member of the Governor-General's Council, or as an adviser called in by various States to re-organise their administrations, or as one of the commissioners appointed to deal with the case of Malhar Rao Gaekwar, Rao Raja Sir Dinkar Rao, K. C. S. I., played for many years a prominent part in the public life of India. If he no longer held any official post in Scindia's State, he at least had laid the foundations of modern Gwalior.

Jayaji Rao and his *Diwan* were both men of strong wills, and those wills had clashed. To his dying day the Maharaja appears to have regarded the respect shown to Dinkar Rao in British India and the honours showered on him as a personal, if an unintentional, affront to his dignity as the Ruler of Gwalior. The very correctness of the ex-minister's attitude—for Dinkar Rao made no complaint—galled his late master's pride.

The feeling thus engendered in the Prince's mind, a feeling doubtless fostered by unworthy advisers in their fear lest the great Brahmin might return to power, was from 1860 onwards reflected in a definite opposition to the enlightened policy which had been inaugurated by the *ex-Diwan.*

Possibly too one effect of the troublous time through which Jayaji Rao had just passed had been to stifle certain liberal administrative views with which between 1854 and 1857 he had been imbued by Dinkar Rao.

In later life, the Maharaja, though he never consulted his ex-minister on matters of internal State policy, on occasion made use of his influence with the British Government to avoid inconvenient notice being taken of certain private scrapes in which he had the misfortune to get entangled.

Two instances may be quoted as illustrative of Jayaji Rao's peculiarities and of the change of vision that the last fifty years have brought about. In each it was expedient to cast a veil over matters which might have developed into undignified scandals. Tradition relates that on one occasion the Maharaja towards the end of a late night ordered the assemblage of his whole army with a view to an immediate attack on Gopal Rao Govind. This tactless officer of the Darbar had dared to deliver to his master a long sermon on the need for the introduction of various administrative reforms!

The earnest solicitation of certain of Jayaji Rao's companions secured the order for the withdrawal of the State Forces after their advance as far as Gola-ka-Mandir, but the Resident as well as the General commanding the British cantonment at Morar failed to appreciate the necessity for the sudden expedition, especially as it had given rise to most disturbing rumours in Lashkar.

Thanks to Dinkar Rao's tact, the matter was allowed to be forgotten.

A similar result followed the ex-minister's intercession in a case where Jayaji Rao enraged by an insult from an individual resident in British India (and so presumably safe from punishment), armed himself and, with a few chosen followers, rode into British territory, attacked the house of his enemy, gave him a sound thrashing, and got back unnoticed to his State before dawn. The victim of the attack—he had been almost cudgelled to death—complained, and awkward explanations resulted.

It was due to Dinkar Rao that this last invasion of British India by an armed force from Gwalior finds no record in the journals of the time.

The end of the Mutiny had found Scindia unwilling to brook the real or fancied predominance of any minister.

Dinkar Rao, the Brahman, was succeeded first by Balaji Chimanji, his Brahman assistant but a mere nonentity, and then in 1868 on Balaji's retirement by Ganpat Rao Khadke. He was no Brahman, indeed not even a Maratha of good parentage but a man who had started life as a palace menial or Huzuria. At the moment British India was ringing with Dinkar Rao's praises, Jayaji Rao is reported to have said that he would show the world that Dinkar Rao was no necessity to Gwalior as its *Diwan*. He would make a Huzuria a *Diwan* to prove his point!

The appointment of so undistinguished an individual to the post of chief minister, an office which in spite of, or through, his utter unscrupulousness Khadke retained until Jayaji Rao's demise, was most ill-advised. For all his mean birth, Khadke was an able man, but his capacity was centred solely on his own unworthy ends. So long as he could please his master by pandering to his whims and vagaries, he was free to amass wealth for himself, and satisfy his private spites and mean ambitions generally.

Those Gwalior Sardars, who on the withdrawal of Dinkar Rao had expected to resume the important *rôle* they had once played in State politics, soon found that they had exchanged King Log for King Stork. By intermarriage between members of their families and those of the ex-Huzuria, alliances dictated by motives

was an intuitive soldier who took a deep interest in the principles of strategy and tactics and sedulously played the war game with his senior military officers. Genuinely interested in soldiering, he was never so happy as when with his troops—the first of each month saw a parade of all the rank and file—or when, watching manœuvres in British India. Were another mutiny to come, he had no intention of being once more deserted by his battalions. Loyally he would fight side by side with his allies, the British, and (since opportunity would doubtless offer), increase his territories at the expense of any of his weaker and less faithful neighbours.

Influenced by these considerations and an exaggerated fear of some fresh disturbance comparable with that of the years 1857-58, the Maharaja amassed money to the neglect of his State. In modern times at all events an administration run on the cheap is foredoomed to failure; it is indeed more harmful than no administration at all. As it was, Jayaji Rao hoarded for an emergency that never came.

It is true that in some of his public works, especially in the erection of palaces, big and small, and the construction of certain reservoirs, he displayed much interest. On this side of his activities, he was ably assisted by Colonel, later Sir, Michael Filose, a grandson of the famous Jean Baptiste, and a most competent architect and engineer as well as a sound civil administrator. In spite of the intrigues of the *Diwan*, Sir Michael always retained the confidence of Jayaji Rao whose playmate he had been in boyhood and whose flight to Agra during the Mutiny he had shared.

Meanwhile the pressing need of the State was improved communications, and especially roads, but the Maharaja objected to their construction on the naive excuse that, should he build them, his subjects might leave Gwalior for British India, if indeed these approaches would not facilitate the invasion of his dominions!

Of grim, almost of awe-inspiring, appearance Jayaji Rao could still be generously appreciative of personal service done to him. "I am not a bard to sing a man's praises. I am a Prince to reward him. How do you know that I have not already done so amply?" was his dignified retort to a presumptuous person who ventured the remark that a certain officer's work in connection with a Viceregal visit had not been eulogised by the Maharaja.

To Sir Lepel Griffin who hinted that Jayaji Rao did not show him the personal affection he had displayed towards Sir Henry Daly the curt reply was immediately forthcoming "First become a Daly."

Many of the Gwalior *Jagirs*, those grants of estates to officers and nobles, date from the time of Jayaji Rao. These gifts of State lands were not given indiscriminately;

the aim of the Ruler was to build up in his territories an aristocracy with a stake in the country. Gwalior had ceased to look towards the Deccan, but its Maratha community was a small one and needed strengthening against reprisals from the petty Rajput holders whose ancestors had been ejected from their lands at the beginning of the nineteenth century.

Yet his Maratha kinsmen had to act strictly in accordance with the law and established usage of the time. If they did not (it was a common saying of his) he, as Jayaji Rao their castefellow, would bewail their punishment but, as Maharaja, he would shed no tears. He would bring them sternly to book.

In this, as in all matters, he was a man of his word.

There is considerable truth, if not complete accuracy in the following passage from Kipling's sketch, "A King's Ashes."

"In his life-time the Maharaja had a deep and rooted distrust of his own family and clan, and no Scindia was ever allowed office about him. Indeed, so great was his aversion that he would not even permit them to die in the Lashkar, or City of Gwalior. They must needs go out when their last hour came, and die in a neighbouring *Jagir* village which belonged to Sir Michael Filose, one of that Italian family which has served the State so long and faithfully. When such a one had died, Scindia by his own command, was not informed of the event till the prescribed days of mourning had elapsed. Then notice was given to him by the placing of his bed on the ground,—a sign of mourning,—and he would ask, not too tenderly, which Scindia is dead ?"

In his private tastes Jayaji Rao was a great patron of the arts of his country and took a special interest in music and painting. He was no student of books but he kept himself closely informed of the progress of events in the outside world through the medium of the Anglo-Indian press, extracts from which in translation were read aloud to him daily. His amusements were much those of other Princes of his time. He was fond of tiger shooting and elephant fights, of wrestling and various exhibitions of physical strength which with his huge frame he could well appreciate; he found pleasure too in frequent gambling parties where a plentiful supply of Indian or European liquor was always in evidence.

As ruler of Gwalior, he considered as political essentials three things, a strong army, a plentiful store of treasure, and the most cordial of relations with the Supreme Power in India. No details referring to other matters interested him in the slightest degree.

In 1862 he had received a Sanad of adoption of which on the death of his third infant son he made use in 1865. Ranoji Scindia, a boy from the Deccan, was brought to Gwalior and recognised as "*Chhota Maharaj*" or heir. In 1870, by consent of the Government of India, this adoption was set aside. The "*Chhota Maharaj*," anxious to snatch the reins of power before his time, had been involved in a plot to poison his adoptive father and had even confessed to his complicity.

On a pension, this vain-headed lad spent the rest of his days in the Deccan whence he had originally come. To judge from the incapacity he showed in life as a private individual, the State has every reason to rejoice that this worthless scion of the house of Scindia never succeeded to the Gwalior *Gadi* with all the manifold responsibilities inherent in that unenviable position.

A plot to poison the Chief—a palace menial as *Diwan*—an administration that was a hundred years behind the times—Gwalior was making little or no apparent progress. Yet men were forgetting the evil days of the Mutiny and ceasing to anticipate its recurrence with each successive spring, although the possibility of such a catastrophe was a common topic of discussion between Jayaji Rao and his immediate *entourage*. The year 1872 gave rise to an abundant crop of local rumours, thanks to the appearance in Gwalior of a lunatic who maintained that he was Nana Sahib of mutiny fame and begged Jayaji Rao to act as a mediator between himself and the British Government!

While he seldom toured in his own State, the Maharaja often visited British India and constantly stayed for a few days at a house he owned in Agra. Even if he occasionally gave vent to his feelings of resentment at some real or imagined slight shown him by some tactless individual Englishman, Jayaji Rao had a genuine appreciation of those highly placed British officers with whom he liked to consort during his absences from Gwalior.

His passionate loyalty to the Supreme Government led him in 1860 and again 1871 to accept various territorial exchanges with an outward fair grace, but it is more than doubtful whether he relished the surrender of his claims to tracts which his forefathers had held in the Deccan.

He had learned to value the railway as a means of quick conveyance and in 1872, from the superfluity of his hoardings, he loaned a sum of seventy-five lakhs of rupees for the construction of the Agra-Gwalior portion of the Indian Midland Railway and a year later a similar amount for the Indore-Neemuch section of the Rajputana-Malwa line.

Lashkar, his capital, certainly merited railway communication with some trunk line of British India. From the mere standing camp (as its name implies) of Doulat Rao, first occupied in 1810, the city had in its sixty years of life grown to be a place of considerable importance; yet of an importance attained not only at the expense of old Gwalior which it had used as a stone quarry but of all the other towns in the State.

Ujjain was languishing in neglect since Lashkar was the centre to which most of the available currency of Gwalior was drawn in each year by the collection of land revenue and custom duties. The bankers of Lashkar found a considerable and profitable business as exchangers of Imperial coin with the Hali, the Chandori, and the Top-shahi rupees, a trio of local and debased issues, then current in the State.

Notwithstanding the revenue reforms introduced by Dinkar Rao in his attempt at land settlement in 1853, certain outlying districts of the State were still farmed out surreptitiously to contractors who paid a fixed sum down for the privilege of squeezing what they could from the wretched cultivators. An opportunity to share in such a profitable business necessitated the continual presence at Lashkar of all would-be contractors so that, as occasion offered and bribes were adequate, this nefarious and theoretically condemned system might be quietly extended once more.

The *jagirs* of the Sardars were seldom visited by their owners who preferred the comparative ease of the capital to the hazards of the districts where life and property were far from safe. Such estates in the early 'seventies were still usually let out each year to the highest bidder except for a few *jagirs* which were systematically rackrented by the holder's personal attention or, in the case of certain absentee landlords, by their merciless stewards.

The favour of a Sardar or high official was held to be of such importance that Lashkar money merchants were prepared to make tremendous advances (naturally at exorbitant rates) to any such prominent personage. As a result of these financial facilities, most of the gentry at the capital were overspending their incomes and living on credit.

This common habit is recorded in a mocking Urdu quatrain still current in the State. A free translation runs:—

"In Jhansi trade is strangled,
In Datia weighted down;
While credit can be wangled,
Never leave Lashkar town."

Without a road worthy of the name, so much so that the Dassera procession, with its gorgeous pageant of gaily painted and caparisoned elephants pacing two abreast, had to make its way along the bed of the *Jinse Nullah*; with its narrow lanes, the relics of the spaces left between the old lines of huts built as temporary shelters for Doulat Rao's soldiery, Lashkar was generally considered by its inhabitants as a delectable place of residence in the 'seventies of the last century.

What if drains there were none? What if few bazars save the picturesque Sarafa, the bankers' quarter, were of any width, or if the streets were no metalled thoroughfares, though in a few places big slabs of stone had been used for paving purposes? For all this Lashkar in those days fully satisfied the civic ideals of the majority of its householders.

In the capital there was at all times abundant material for gossip; almost daily some new rumour sped on its course retailing which officer or Sardar was in momentary favour with the Darbar, and which in disgrace, or narrating the latest vagaries of their Ruler who for all his inaccessibility could not fail to impress his subjects by the pomp he displayed at the numerous religious festivals.

The latest court intelligence, true or false, was of absorbing interest to a town population, the majority of which owed their actual food and drink, indeed their whole parasitic existence to the palace and the swollen establishments of the Sardars.

The rumour emanating from the Hanuman Temple one evening might be that the Maharaja had lost his temper with Khadke, "the Karbari Sahib." Would the result be an open rupture? The shrewder students of parochial politics would decide against any such suggestion: holding rightly, that the minister would get round his master just as he had so often done before.

Or a discussion would take place about the new palace which "Mukhel Sahib," *i.e.*, Sir Michael Filose, was just then building for the Maharaja. To test the strength of the arched Darbar Hall their Ruler had ordered elephants to perambulate upon its roof. That was a clever idea, was it not? Who but a King, such as theirs, would have ever thought of it?

Or again two Sardars whose days for interference in the administration of the State had long passed might have puffed into flames the embers of some traditional family feud. In instant response their servants, the self-appointed keepers of their respective master's honour, would start a scuffle in the narrow lanes of Lashkar, and each participant thereafter magnifying the heroic part he had played, would extract some gift of cash or cloth from his lord.

For these hangers-on there was little danger in squabbling and assaulting one another, so long as they did not fall foul of the Huzurias and other super-menials attached to the Maharaja's establishment nor hinder the licensed robbery practised in the grain bazar by the State troops as a relaxation from the strict discipline enforced within cantonment limits.

Persons of independent social views were rare at this time in Lashkar. Nearly everyone was a client of some patron a little bigger than himself. Each day it was his duty to visit his patron, in order to render obeisance and to administer a dose of fulsome, but judicious, flattery. The more a patron rose in the estimation of society, the more was his client's own horn of honour exalted. How happy those who had an *entree* to the precincts of the palace and perhaps might get a chance of paying obeisance to their Ruler from a distance! Eventually they might attract their Prince's notice and even be invited to gamble with him. That was not merely an honour but a profitable amusement; for the man of moderate means could keep his winnings, while, if he lost, he could plead poverty and his debt to the Maharaja would be remitted!

Lashkar was still wallowing in an orgy of pride of birth. A man was not estimated, he did not estimate himself, by what he had done or what was his worth in the world. It was the worth of his ancestors that mattered. Some Ekanda and Siledar, or other irregular trooper might be hopelessly in debt, and might have the monthly cash grant for his maintenance mortgaged years ahead, but he still was a "Khasa" (a special one) and a Maratha at that. His forbears had been great men when Mahadji rode to Delhi. He was of the same caste as the Maharaja, perhaps even a distant relation of some Sardar at whose house he could always scrape a meal, if the larder at home were empty.

What if his circumstances were narrow, while his great-grandfather had bulged with loot? He knew all the tricks of old Maratha horsemanship. In his pride he would gallop his weedy country-bred down some narrow lane and raise the curses of those wayfarers whose lives were endangered by his exhibition. What did that matter? They were only pedestrians, he a cavalry-man whose forefathers had played their part in countless battles, so many indeed that it was impossible to recall the names of any one of them!

In Lashkar, fifty years ago, everyone who possessed a mount of any sort usually rode, unless he were carried in a palanquin. The city's potholed, tortuous lanes were ill-suited for any wheeled conveyance save the sturdiest of springless bullock carts. The nonchalant Sardar would take an evening airing on his elephant, while the lesser gentry clattered about on horseback better mounted by far than the irregular State cavalry on their narrow-chested, sickle-hocked country-breds. The man who could afford no horse of any kind might at least be perched aloft a gurgling camel, an animal that cost nothing to feed, but one which most Brahmins considered forbidden to them by their caste rules as well as by their sense of dignity.

The houses of the Sardars were the chief centres for the amusements beloved of the populace. Into the courtyards of such residences, indeed inside the actual buildings, would edge a large number of uninvited guests when a nautch party, a wrestling match, or a quail or partridge fight was afoot. Even if they were not personally known to the big man of the house, at least they felt that by their presence at the spectacle they had been near to greatness!

Such were some of the joys of life in Lashkar where, in spite of moderately good wells, cholera became endemic each summer when the melons and the hot weather arrived simultaneously. Throughout each month of the twelve malaria took its usual toll, and infant mortality among all classes, high and low, spared but few of the children born.

Thanks to the difficulty of exporting from the State the surplus of the harvests, food, however, was cheap. Even in 1880 after the railway had begun to carry away super-abundant stocks, *juar* was still sold at thirty-four and wheat at twenty-four seers to the rupee. Perhaps that is the main reason for the common belief among the poorer classes in Lashkar to-day that the two decades following the Mutiny were their city's golden age.

Such was the civilisation of the capital. In the districts, and especially in those remote from head-quarters, conditions were far wilder.

There the Rajputs who were mostly petty land-holders but who outnumbered their Maratha masters by not less than fifteen to one would have risen in open revolt but for their innate incapacity for combination and their fear of the disciplined troops at the disposal of the State.

Since Dinkar Rao's first settlement, the revenue had usually been collected without the aid of bayonets, always without the use of cannon, but still commonly with the help of a big stick. It was rarely paid up without some form of coercion, prestige demanding at least a show of superior force.

Although the Rajputs openly made no common cause against the administration, they in their turn preyed on others weaker than themselves and countered oppression with lawlessness. Things were not so desperate as they had been in the days of Pindaris, yet dacoity and crimes of violence were of daily occurrence in every district of the State.

While they seldom enlisted in Scindia's Army, the poorer of the Rajputs came forward as recruits for the police, a service that gave them an official screen behind which to carry out their depredations or to connive at robbery and murder. The police force in each district was under the control of the *Suba*, *i. e.*, the collector, but in spite of the fact that some *Subas* were honest men and not mere creatures of the *Diwan*, the constabulary and their superior officers paid little attention to the protection of any life and property beyond their own.

The supreme test of efficiency in a *Suba*, as estimated at the capital, was the regularity with which he forwarded his fixed quota of revenue to the treasury at Lashkar. Knowing this, his chief pre-occupation was the collection of the annual dues and the steadily accumulating arrears claimed by the State from its needy cultivators, though he seldom forget to line his own pockets in the process!

In his *zila* or district the *Suba* was for practical purposes supreme. On his tours through his *zila* he was always accompanied by a considerable escort of armed men as well as by a large retinue of State and private servants, not to mention minor officials most of whom regarded the *ryot* as their legitimate prey.

A *Suba's* duties as head of the district police were to his thinking a very minor concern, since he was not only a revenue officer but also the head of the *zila* court. Having seldom received any legal training, he was usually unfitted for the post of a wise, as well as an upright, judge. Such a disqualification, however, was of little moment, for the law courts generally, not excluding those at the capital, were neither honest nor efficient.

Though Jayaji Rao never interfered personally with the course of such justice as was administered, his *Diwan* is credited with no such scruples. On innumerable occasions Khadke is reported to have set aside any decisions which clashed with his personal wishes or convenience or in which, on appeal to him, the loser in a suit might tender a bigger bribe than the victor.

Distressing as may be this record of the mismanagement, insecurity, and dishonesty prevailing in the Gwalior State less than half a century ago, it is but fair to the generation now alive that the truth should be stated, if not stressed. In no way is it intended to convey the impression that all the State officials of that time were equally incapable or corrupt. On the contrary, throughout the whole of Gwalior to this day the names of certain holders of high posts are still remembered with gratitude as men who did justice and checked extortion in spite of the intrigues of the *Diwan* against them.

As a whole the inhabitants of Gwalior knew nothing better than their unfortunate state. The majority were unusually ignorant even for those times; since very little money was doled out for education (in 1870 the total grant for this purpose was under twenty thousand rupees) and few could read or write any language beyond their own vernacular.

English was a rare accomplishment. A clerk who later rose to be a prominent civil officer owed his earliest advancement from a minor subordinate post to his aptitude for translating into vernacular the English telegrams then beginning to reach Lashkar.

To his credit be it said that his translations were usually correct!

In connection with the large buildings in course of erection during the 'seventies under the supervision and according to the designs, of Sir Michael Filose, a certain amount of elementary technical education imparted in English was becoming a necessity. From the money sanctioned for the construction of the Jai Bilas Palace (an edifice completed in time for the residence of the late King-Emperor during his three days' visit to Gwalior as Prince of Wales). Sir Michael started a class to train overseers among the local youth. In later life some of the students from this class proved themselves able officers in various administrative lines.

Except for the opium grown for the China market, the State had as yet developed little external trade. The natural export of surplus agricultural produce from Gwalior was hopelessly hampered by vexatious custom duties levied on goods in passage from one district of the State to another and by the general lack of metalled roads and bridges, as well as by the ever present danger of loot and highway robbery.

After making every allowance for exaggeration, it must be admitted that in the 'seventies Gwalior was in a deplorable state.

Nor was the condition of its ruler more enviable. Of the many things which Jayaji Rao neglected in life his own health was one. In spite of the retention of considerable physical strength, ere he reached his fortieth year, his habitual excesses had undermined a naturally tough constitution. While three daughters, the issue of his first three wives, had lived, three sons had died in infancy. His adopted son had proved a traitor and deservedly had been banished from Gwalior. His Sardars and other advisers in social matters, the court astrologers, and his own inclinations urged him to marry yet again.

In 1875 his choice fell on the daughter of Bapu Sahib Jadho, one of the leading nobles in his State. The bride, who at marriage received the name of Sakhya Raja, was but thirteen years of age, the bridegroom over forty. In February the wedding ceremony was held at Parsen, a village some eleven miles east of Lashkar. Scindia's Army had recently been engaged on manœuvres in the neighbourhood, but the real reason for the selection of so out-of-the-way a spot was that at the moment the Mohurram, that Shia festival of mourning, was being celebrated at the capital. Hindu marriage rejoicings might offend Muslim sentiment and although the Mohammedan population of Gwalior was less than ten per cent of the whole community, that section was far more important than its mere numbers implied. At this period religious riots were no uncommon feature in State politics, though Malwa was more notorious in this respect than Northern Gwalior.

The general festivities, indeed the actual wedding ceremonies, were utterly disorganised by violent winds which levelled to the ground all the *shamianas* and tents erected, except that of Sir Michael Filose, and by hailstones which stampeded elephants, horses, and camels and which with the lapse of years have grown into missiles of enormous size, "as big as flowerpots," to quote one graphic description of an eye witness!

From this unseasonal, this untoward, occurrence the superstitious drew a variety of omens. The Mohurram was an unlucky date for any such joyous celebration as a wedding. For all its Hindu ancestry the Gwalior State from its foundation by the Scindias had been known as the *Musalmani Gadi*, the Mohammedan throne, since the first rulers of its territories had administered the northern provinces in the name of the Moghul Emperor.

Mohammedan Saints too had blessed some of the earlier Scindias. In memory of one such special occasion was not the hereditary religious adviser at the court of the Hindu Maharaja of Gwalior a Muslim?

So far as can be gathered from persons whose fading memories can recall those times, the general sentiment at Lashkar seems to have been that such a marriage could hardly prove a lucky one. Probably it would be fruitless, or, if issue came, it would be yet another girl, not the desired son, or even were it a boy, the child would die in infancy as three boys had died already.

The next eighteen months were memorable in the history of Gwalior for little beyond the visit of His Royal Highness Albert Edward, Prince of Wales. In the first year after his marriage Jayaji Rao paid various visits to British India, but thereafter he stayed chiefly at his capital. In accordance with his usual habit while in Lashkar, he spent a week or so at one of his palaces or pleasure houses and the next few days at another.

The *Urs*, or ceremony commemorative of Mansur Shah Sahib, the Muslim Saint, who had blessed Mahadji Scindia and the descendants of whose disciple were the hereditary religious guides of the Maharajas of Gwalior, was celebrated as usual in the Gorkhi or State temple at Lashkar. At this annual celebration held in a Hindu shrine the Scindia of the day has to sit until some of the heaped-up flowers placed under a turban fall on his lap.

Such a fall of flowers is called a *Prasad* or divine gift. Once the fall has occurred, there are shouts of joy from the spectators, and the astrologers announce the prospects for the Ruler during the ensuing year.

Jayaji Rao sat at the Gorkhi but, in spite of his having fasted, nothing happened on the first day. No petals fell. There was no *Prasad*. Undaunted, he continued fasting and sat again the next day.

Suddenly the whole heap of flowers with the turban on top of them fell into his lap. This was a *Maha Prasad*, a super-gift, such as was rarely bestowed. The hopes for luck during the next twelvemonth were rosy. The year 1876 should prove a most fortunate one for the house of Scindia.

About the middle of October the Maharaja was stopping at the Jai Bilas Palace for which building, though the most imposing of his residences he cared but little. His young wife Sakhya Raja, or "Jija Maharaj" as she was commonly called, was staying at her father's house in Lashkar.

On the 20th of the month about eleven o'clock at night the fourteen year old Maharani gave birth to a son. Salvos of cannon and musket shots were fired. In his spacious Darbar Hall Jayaji Rao received the congratulations of his Sardars and high officers.

Lavish provision was made for public feastings and general rejoicings. With the utmost vagueness of which their lore is capable, the court astrologers began their task of drawing the horoscope of the infant, Madhav Rao Scindia.

Jayaji Rao's devotion had been rewarded. A *Maha Prasad* had fallen into his lap, and the super-gift had proved to be the birth of a son. In his "Policy," written nearly fifty years later, that son naively points out the happy coincidence.

CHAPTER III.

1876–1886

WEIN, a marked partiality for the "Raja's peg" of brandy with a dash of champagne in place of soda-water, *Weib*, whereon a veil must needs be thrown, and *Gesang*, endless nautch parties at which any distinction between day and night disappeared, such were the chief amusements, nay the very occupations, of Maharaja Jayaji Rao. The environment of his father's court itself was no ideal one in which the young Prince should be reared.

In the beginning, however, it seemed unlikely that Madhav Rao Scindia ever would grow up from infancy to boyhood; for the first two years of his life at least constant doubts as to his power to survive were whispered at the palace.

But the devoted care of the girl-mother was shrewd, and by the time he had reached his third year, the baby boy, if still somewhat short for his age, had developed into a sturdy youngster with a well-knit frame. Physically at all events he looked tough enough to tackle the serious business of life that lay before him.

From the first, according to the custom of the time, "the *Chhota Maharaj*" was surrounded with a big retinue of palace servants, for the most part servile flatterers to whose interest it was that their future master should grow up no whit better or wiser than the least distinguished of his ancestors. The instinct of self-preservation in such parasites dictated their constant inculcation of the creed:—

"Why turn out the old?
Why bring in the new?
What suited your forebears
Surely should suit you."

Madhav Rao Scindia's first five years were largely spent in the zenana, where in those days the *purdah* was a strict reality and not the mere form into which he later turned it. Within its seclusion he found his best playmate in his mother.

He never forgot those hours of play; he never lost the play habit. Until her death in 1919, he would, when wearied out by work at office files or other State duties, pay a visit to his mother's quarters and, sitting on the ground beside her, play with her almost as they both had played two score years before.

One incident which occurred when he was about four calls for mention, since in it we can trace the origin of a peculiarity which had tragic results in later life. A minor juvenile operation was necessary, and Maharaja Jayaji Rao who had recognised the value of western medical science in the relief it afforded him in his sufferings from the dropsy which at length killed him, summoned from Indore an English surgeon. The doctor gave "the Chhota Maharaj" a whiff of chloroform and made the necessary cut. The trifling operation was quite successful, and the child passed easily from unconsciousness to sleep; but one or more palace servants who objected to modern surgery lied to their young master. He had nearly died under the anæsthetic, they affirmed: with difficulty their prayers and devotion had saved him. The inhibition thus started in the child became as he grew up an unreasonable aversion to the use of the surgeon's knife and its humane preliminary whether chloroform or ether.

From the age of five or so the young Prince began to move more freely in the world around him. The Phul Bagh, the park surrounding the Jai Bilas and Moti Mahal Palaces, was in those days divided into many sections by countless walls and gates. Madhav Rao Scindia was fond of exploration. Gradually the orbit of his wanderings widened. In the end his strayings brought him to the outer wall of all. He was alone, having dodged all his attendants. He came to the last gate. The guard on duty wished to stop him from going outside. He stamped his little foot, but they quoted his father's orders and were adamant.

He retired, but refused to allow one of them to accompany him. After a minute or so, he returned running. "The Maharaja Sahib is coming," he shouted. "He goes to Morar." The guard drew up in line to do obeisance to their ruler. In an instant the boy had slipped through the open gate and stood outside laughing at them. "My father goes to Morar to-morrow," he cried.

It is the first recorded instance of Madhav Rao Scindia playing a practical joke. Delighted with his success, he returned inside the gate and went back to the palace. Again he refused an escort and, when the guard were insistent, repeated his refusal in the firmest of tones. Already he had acquired the power to issue orders in a way that brooked of no disobedience. In Lashkar it was common knowledge that the future ruler of Gwalior clearly possessed the imperious disposition to be expected as a part of Nature's dower to an Indian prince. From the capital a rumour to this effect spread all over the State. When "*the Chhota Maharaj*" gave a command, it had to be obeyed forthwith.

Despite his neglect of his administrative duties, Maharaja Jayaji Rao was a strong character; despite his waste of his great physical and mental powers, he was a man of iron will; despite his inattention to the crying needs of his subjects, he had a personality of considerable charm; and these distinguishing features he transmitted in increased force to his son.

As regards the Maharani Sakhya Raja or "Jija Maharaj" (to use the affectionate title under which her memory is still revered) there is a general impression current that she was a lady gifted with great administrative powers. This idea would seem to rest on no basis of administrative achievement. More probably it results from the fact that during the later years of her son's minority she received from the Government of India the title of "Regent," a title conferring no powers, and from the further fact that on several occasions she held charge of the State during her son's absences from Gwalior.

But assuming her to have been devoid of any innate aptitude for public affairs (she had little chance of an acquired aptitude) she will long live in the hearts of the people of Gwalior. There is never a story told of her which does not show her to have been not merely a kind-hearted but a great-hearted woman, and one too possessed of an infinite capacity for patient suffering, whether mental or physical. Her influence and her advice—the latter after her son's attainment of his majority was never given unasked—were always on the side of the angels, in support of mercy, liberality, and compassion.

A kindly nature Madhav Rao Scindia acquired from his mother at birth; to her early training are due various lovable traits which developed in his character and especially that lively sympathy with his subjects, whether as individuals or as a whole, and more particularly with those in direst distress.

It was her humanity of disposition and her sense of fair play, rather than her inherited objection as the daughter of a Sardar to an upstart, which from the first led "Jija Maharaj" to object to Khadke, *the Diwan*, and his oppression. The girl Maharani had no influence with her rapidly aging husband, whose temper with the progress of his dropsy was daily becoming more variable. All she could do was to bring up her son as well as a mother's loving shrewdness would allow in spite of all the handicaps of custom and environment. Yet all those whose memories can recall those days, agree that she was opposed to the minister and his dishonest ways. In vain he sought to ingratiate himself with her.

On one occasion in the early 'eighties it seemed that Khadke's fall was at last imminent. Maharaja Jayaji Rao had been paying a visit to the Agent to the Governor-General at Indore, a city not far from Ujjain. Perhaps the notorious peculations of Temak, the brother-in-law of Khadke, and, like the *Diwan*, of Huzuria origin, had been one of the matters discussed between the Chief and the Political Officer. For several years Temak had held the post of *Sar Suba* or chief administrator, in power little less than vice-gerent for Jayaji Rao, in Malwa. That Temak had been an unjust steward was common knowledge; the Maharaja knew it as well as the man in the street notwithstanding all the *Sar Suba's* affection of piety and poverty.

From Indore the Maharaja had just returned to Lashkar. The highest officer in Malwa had been arrested; so people believed. He would be brought in fetters, silver fetters (an imaginative touch) to the capital. Temak's day was over; every one was sure of that. Would he merely be flung into gaol without trial or might even lose his life? Gossip found this speculation of surpassing interest, for it involved the allied question, would Temak's fall bring about with it the overthrow of his near relation, Khadke?

But conjecture proved at fault. Temak arrived at Lashkar, unfettered, but in obvious disgrace. He was forbidden to attend the palace and for weeks was left in uncertainty as to his fate. At last a summons came to him from the Maharaja. All Lashkar was certain that the *Sar Suba* was to be trampled to death by elephants. Perhaps the spectacle would be a public one.

These pleasurable anticipations were, alas! falsified. Terms were propounded to Temak. The amount of the fine imposed on him is variously stated at any sum from fifty lakhs down to five. In any case, the speed with which the fine was paid so pleased the Maharaja that the disgraced officer was re-instated in favour, given a cash reward in open Darbar, and then made a deputy-*diwan* at headquarters!

This, perhaps, the most striking administrative act of Maharaja Jayaji Rao, was also one of the last instances of that Ruler's interference with the dismal routine of internal politics under the corrupt *regime* of his minister and his satellites.

Careless as the Maharaja was of the way in which his State was mal-administered, he was consumed by one private ambition which he yearned to see accomplished before his death. Since the Mutiny the Gwalior Fortress had been in the occupation of British troops, while again but three miles from the capital was the military cantonment of Morar with its large garrison. The restoration of the citadel had been promised by Lord Canning in 1859, so soon as the rendition was considered safe. Hitherto various tentative suggestions that the times were ripe for the return of the Fort had been brusquely or tactfully negatived.

As a faithful ally of the Supreme Power, and, whatever were his failings, Jayaji Rao was certainly that, he keenly felt the indignity of his situation with the cannon on the fortress dominating his capital and indeed his palace. What if those cannon on occasion thundered out his salute or if his flag flew from the ramparts? In his heart rankled the tactless jest of a British officer who had pointed out that, if necessary, the Jai Bilas and Moti Mahal Palaces could in two minutes be blown to bits by the big guns on the bastions of "the pearl in the necklace of the castles of Hind." Since the day on which that joke had been made, Jayaji Rao had never again visited the citadel.

Sir Dinkar Rao's help is reported to have been enlisted to achieve the consummation of a desire which the Maharaja had first openly expressed a full two decades earlier. Happily the year 1885 saw the fulfilment of the old promise. In exchange for Jhansi, a town then included in the Gwalior State, and a payment of fifteen lakhs for the barracks at Morar, that cantonment and the Gwalior Fortress were restored to Scindia.

Until the stronghold was actually evacuated—the event did not take place until the following spring—the Maharaja refused to enter the historic citadel over which for nearly thirty years he had exercised no control. Sir Michael Filose, however, was consulted with regard to a gigantic engineering project, namely the construction of an enormous causeway to lead from the Jai Bilas Palace to the south end of the Fort some three hundred feet above.

By the time that the last British soldier had marched away to the tune of "Tommy, make room for your uncle," Jayaji Rao was too ill to visit the possession which after so many years had been restored to him. In vain each day he hoped that on the morrow he could bear the fatigue of the proposed trip; he consoled his chagrin at his weakness by the thought that at least the citadel would be his son's.

And meanwhile what of that son?

From his first expedition beyond the precincts of the Moti Mahal Palace the boy had shown manifest signs of precocity. Madhav Rao Scindia never read Peter the Great's life, but on his far smaller stage he in many ways resembled the Muscovite. At the age of seven the Maratha Prince is reported to have commented on the order and cleanliness of the Morar Cantonment as opposed to the muddle and dirt of Lashkar, much as two centuries earlier the great Russian had contrasted the neat German Faubourg outside the walls of Moscow with the picturesque, but slovenly, nightmare of the Kremlin within.

To give an anecdote resting on the excellent testimony:—

"The Chhota Maharaj's" hair was being cut and the enforced inactivity during the operation had been very trying to the boy who was never happy unless running here and there. At last the wearisome business was over, the hair cut, the side-locks by the ears trimmed in true Maratha fashion. It had been a slow job, and the boy was telling the barber so when his father entered. Jayaji Rao suggested that the barber might be rewarded by a gift of clothes. Such a proposal was too much,

From the child it evoked the retort that in his opinion the fellow deserved no special recognition. Earnestly the son impressed on his sire his view of the case. Was not the hair-cutter a laggard at his work? And in any case was he not well paid for his services? Madhav Rao Scindia undertook, if necessary, to provide his father with a barber who would perform his duties just as well, and for half the salary!

A vignette with the correctness of its details fully vouched for:—There was a garden party given in the "Company Bagh" at Agra. Lord and Lady Ripon were present and mingling with the crowd of notabilities from the neighbourhood who had collected for the occasion. Seeing "the Chhota Maharaj" for the first time, the Vicereine asked the boy through the medium of Colonel Tweedie, then the Resident at Gwalior, why he had not accompanied his father when that Chief had had an audience with the Viceroy earlier in the day. The child's reply was quick; he did not pay visits without a personal invitation. Amused by the reply, Her Excellency promised to send him some toys from Bombay whither she was shortly bound. The promise elicited an immediate response. He would like the toys there and then. Were there no shops in Agra? When people went to Bombay, they forgot things! Though still ignorant of the proverb (a later favourite) "a bird in the hand," he evidently had learned its truth, for, until the Vicereine had repeated her promise and Colonel Tweedie had guaranteed its performance, he refused to be convinced. Eventually two big boxes of toys arrived from Bombay.

Such trifling incidents from Madhav Rao Scindia's childhood are quoted not because they are of any absorbing interest, but merely since they show that, as a boy, he was already displaying traits which became marked in his character as a man.

Outward slovenliness except in dress always irritated him. Work must be quick, and a Ruling Prince should not pay more than a commoner for ordinary services rendered to him. If he wanted anything particularly, Scindia usually gambled for a quick return, even if patience promised one more profitable. In spite of his constant quotation of the adage "Rome was not built in a day," the truth conveyed in the words never gave him any satisfaction.

Like Peter the Great too, in his tastes he was mechanically-minded from the first. He always liked to see "the wheels go round," still more to discover the cause for their revolution. Like a magnet the State Workshops would draw him and so would Sir Michael Filose's house with its models of machines as well as its telescopes to be looked through. Before he was eight he had clambered on to the footplate of a locomotive at the Gwalior Station and tried to cajole the driver into letting him take the engine to Agra!

That afternoon, it is said, caused consternation to his attendants. His mother hid the escapade from his father, but Khadke reported it, though happily the *Diwan's* suggestion that such behaviour must be due to the bad influence of Sir Michael Filose had no result. To-day there seems nothing extraordinary in this childish expression of the usual English boy's dream of being an engine driver; but in Gwalior forty odd years ago such an aspiration on the lips of a youthful Maratha Prince was doubtless regarded as a firmament-shaking enormity.

Possibly the court astrologers congratulated themselves on having drawn "the Chhota Maharaj's" horoscope with such vagueness. Who could tell into what such a boy might develop? Certainly even the most prescient of them never anticipated that in later years they would often see their Ruler lying in the dust under his own or another's motor car and tinkering with its mechanism; still less that they would come to regard such a sight as an everyday occurrence and might, perhaps, be asked to hand Madhav Maharaj some tool and then get a sarcastic rebuke for not knowing the difference between a spanner and a turnscrew.

From his earliest days it was obvious that the young Prince had inherited much of his father's love of military matters. The toy model of a fortress built for his amusement just outside the Moti Mahal Palace has now for years past been utilised as a part of the main offices of the State. The particular site chosen for the miniature citadel was probably selected because in his later years Jayaji Rao spent much of his time at the Moti Mahal. The extensive block of buildings comprised under that name had been constructed entirely after his wishes. More or less an accurate copy of the Peshwa's palace at Poona, Jayaji Rao as its originator, ever preferred it to Jai Bilas which contrary to common belief ante-dates the so-called "older palace" by a year or two.

One story told of Madhav Rao Scindia's youth relates that when only seven he insisted that certain hanging fans being put up in a room at Moti Mahal were being set to pull the wrong way. Unless they were hung to swing across the room at right angles to their original direction, the puller's energy would be wasted and the amount of breeze produced would be practically nil. The reply that they had always been hung in one particular direction did not satisfy him. An enquiry into his theory proved it to be right in practice.

In later years, in connection alike with the location of the State offices in Moti Mahal as with various structural alterations to the building, he was destined time and again to prove himself more practical than either his officers or the two committees to which he had originally entrusted the work. One of the sights of Lashkar to-day is the arrangement by which the sights of Lashkar today is the arrangement by which the principal government offices are accommodated with due regard to economy of space and time, and to general efficiency. The arrangement was almost entirely the child of "Madhav Maharaj's" own brain, and was one of the last works in which he showed for the moment that on occasions that brain could still be as practical as it had been when his mental powers shone at their zenith.

With his health rapidly decaying, Jayaji Rao came to pass more and more of his time at Moti Mahal. Though he retained his idiosyncrasy of spending a few days at one residence and then a few days at another, Moti Mahal was the place to which he came back after each excursion. It was rumoured that much of his hoarded wealth was hidden in secret subterranean vaults at Moti Mahal, a supposition resting on a certain basis of fact.

The once favourite palace at Kampoo Kothi, hard by the Lashkar Cantonment where most of the State troops were quartered, was now seldom visited. Neglected too lay that rambling block of buildings much of which dated back to the days of Doulat Rao, the huge Maharajwara, right in the centre of Lashkar. Even if Jayaji Rao was not in residence at Moti Mahal, his son and his son's mother would usually be there.

The failing health of the Maharaja made it of little avail to suggest reforms, even if such suggestions arrived with the high backing of brusque or tactful hints from the Government of India. However backward the Gwalior State might be in times that refused to stand still, it was recognised by one Resident after another that little in the way of improvement in administration could be looked for yet awhile. Khadke as *Diwan* was as supreme as ever. With his title of "Rao Raja" and a K. C. S. I. he had imposed on Gwalior the myth that he was as useful to the British Government as to his master!

The one hope of Gwalior was "the Chhota Maharaj." Tutors he had from the age of six, but it is doubtful if, with all his quickness, he acquired much in the shape of book learning from his first pedagogues. In no way studious, his tastes ran rather to doing things than to reading about them.

From the beginning he was set too many languages to learn at one time. First there was Marathi, a tongue which few of the State-born Marathas could speak or write correctly. Still necessarily he must learn that, the vernacular of his race. Then there was Urdu with its Persian characters. As the language of the law courts, the need for the study of Urdu could not be gainsaid. And, thirdly, there was Hindi. Even if the high Brij Bhasha literature were never mastered, some knowledge of Hindi must be acquired. The Pundits too put in a word for Sanskrit, that sacred classic with all its perfections and complications. Sanskrit, even if not fully comprehended, was a fitting subject in the education of any Prince who was a Hindu. There was merit in its study.

Lastly there was English, the new burden that changed times had imposed on Indian school-boys. For persons born to high positions English was not without value. It was undoubtedly an advantage if a Maharaja could speak to a Viceroy or Resident or some other high British official in English and so dispense with the services of an interpreter who might deceive him.

The natural result was that, while (with the exception of Sanskrit) Madhav Rao Scindia acquired a working knowledge of all these tongues, he was never really proficient in any of them. So far as English at least was concerned, his imperfect knowledge of the meaning of some word or phrase occasionally led him to misconstrue the import of some remark in conversation or in a letter, and once or twice in his life with unfortunate results.

But, though, when in the Deccan, he had to apologise for his inability to speak Marathi of any purity, though his Urdu was never "high Urdu," and his Hindi did not allow him to comprehend any of the beauties of the Ramayana or Mahabharata, he hammered out for practical purposes two rather virile dialects of his own, one based on simple Urdu but written in *Modi, i. e.,* Marathi cursive characters, the other largely a hotch-potch of English slang and colloquialisms.

In later life he proved an effective speaker whether after preparation or impromptu, in either of these two linguistic inventions, or in a mixture of both, a mixture that was most telling when he wished to speak out his mind to his subjects.

Yet, though his education was but starting, and though too much in the way of languages was being attempted for his age, and that attempted on faulty lines, his natural intelligence and his unusual power of observation were noticeable by all who came in contact with him.

It seems that the late Maharaja Madhav Rao Scindia was fully conscious that an attempt had been made during his tender years to teach him too many tongues at once.

His reasoned estimate of the drawbacks in his own early education may be gauged from various remarks made by him towards the end of his life when laying down instructions in "The Darbar Policy" for his own son's training. In the first volume of that book undue educational stress before the age of nine is deprecated. Marathi, Urdu, and later English are mentioned as the languages to be studied. Pure Hindi, apart from the hybrid Hindi of Gwalior, *i.e.,* simple Urdu in *Devánagari* characters, is not specified, while no mention is made of Sanskrit.

In "The Darbar Policy" again great stress is laid on the necessity of securing for a young Chief as guardians "sensible, good-natured, well-informed, and respectable people; but it must be seen that they are not so advanced in years that the infirmities of their age keep them from constantly remaining close to the Prince," or, to judge from another extract from sharing in his pursuits and amusements.

As a high-spirited boy, full of life, it is clear that Madhav Rao Scindia had correctly assessed the handicap of guardians whose days for energetic exercise had passed. To judge from the tales of his boyhood such as he often told, he did just what he liked with his early tutors and guardians and, when bored by their ministrations, would make them the victims of practical jokes.

He had noticed too, it may be affirmed, the mistake, indeed the danger, of a large retinue of body-servants. For the present Ruler of Gwalior during his minority the number of his personal attendants has been strictly limited by his father's "Policy." Much insistence is placed on George Jayaji Rao Scindia being able to do things for himself "as no one can say when an occasion may arise when he may have to act alone."

There is wisdom in such injunctions. To this day too many an Indian principality is an autocracy tempered for evil by the wiles of palace menials whose apparent subservience blinds their master to their cunning, to their desire that he grow up vicious. In the weakness they induce in their lord lies their strength. Pimps by heredity and training for the most part, they plot and scheme to ruin any Prince from his earliest years. If he can grow up with an overweening sense of his own importance and a sufficient indifference to the responsibilities of his position, they feel that their servility has not been in vain, for then their duplicity will reap a rich harvest. Collectively they are stronger than any individual tutor or guardian. By suggestion they tempt the young Chief in his leisure hours, aided as they are by an environment the undue stimulus of which only the strongest of characters can resist. Their sole conception of disloyalty is any hesitation in pandering to a boy Prince's every whim. Chiefs come and go, are born and die, abdicate or are deposed, but the palace menials go on for ever. Profuse in their professions of eternal fidelity to the lord who feeds them, they cheat and rob him and his subjects, sell his secrets, induce around him an atmosphere of suspicion, actively oppose honest dealing and straightforwardness, and generally work havoc in a weak Ruler's domestic, social, and political life.

Among their ranks occasionally may be found some individual servitor who is not actively base and, perhaps, one in a thousand who may be held to be a freak, a throw-back to decency as it were; but as a body they are untiring promoters of evil. Individually weak, collectively strong, they lust after power, power to do mischief and power to corrupt. For such a purpose they will intrigue unceasingly and, understanding the advantages of a division of labour, will allow particular individuals to implant in a young Prince the seeds of the special vices in which the savants among them are adept.

This wearisome indictment of Indian palace servants may close with the remark that it applies to either sex and that, as Kipling has said, "the female of the species is more deadly than the male."

In his earlier years the life of Madhav Rao Scindia was in many respects so ordered as to suit the convenience of his father's health. Jayaji Rao was proud of his son, and, when the state of his health permitted, kept him by his side. But the strength of the prematurely aging Maharaja was rapidly declining: he would submit to no regular treatment for his dropsy. His chief medical attendant was one Kasim Khan whose skill is still remembered by old folk in Lashkar, but in his master the physician found an unruly patient who would not diet nor take his medicines for more than a day at a time. The Maharaja was slightly more amenable to the ministrations of a *Sanyasi* who was *sadhoo*, astrologer, and *vaidya* rolled into one. Like his son in later years, Jayaji Rao set no faith in medical men and would grow furious with their regulations. He could not endure to be forced to do anything. For example, Mr. Val Prinsep, the artist, while declaring him to be in physique by far the most powerful Chief he had ever painted, also found him the worse sitter. He complained that His Highness was not steady for a moment.

"If Sir Henry Daly were not here, I would not sit at all" was Jayaji Rao's retort. "This is worse than the hardest day's *puja* I ever had, and, after all, what is the use ? I don't get anything out of it."

Such an answer was just that which his son might have made thirty years later. Madhav Rao Scindia would give no portrait painter a fair chance of showing his skill.

When suffering pain, Jayaji Rao would often try to distract his mind from his agony by recalling every detail of the visit of the Prince of Wales to Gwalior in 1876. He would review every incident of the ceremonial parade of his army and say that on that occasion he had saluted His Royal Highness with his sword, an honour he had paid to no one else in his life. He would talk of the gracious words with which his Royal Guest had praised the Gwalior troops and the skill shown by himself as their commander in conducting the sham fight with which the parade had ended. The formal compliment from the Prince of Wales was valued by Maharaja Jayaji Rao far more highly than the serious remark of Sir William Mansfield, an old Commander-in-Chief, who had said that few brigadiers in the British Army were able to put a division of the three arms through a field day so well as the Maharaja of Gwalior.

Continuing his oft repeated tale, Jayaji Rao would tell of the State banquet held in the Jai Bilas Palace at the conclusion of which he had come in and from an enormous golden goblet, said to contain a magnum of champagne, had drunk the Prince's health. The Prince had listened attentively to the speech he had made, a speech translated into English by his friend, Sir Henry Daly. What was it the Maharaja had said? He would repeat his actual words "I am an ignorant man almost without education. I know nothing of the English language. What I did with the troops is an instance of what can be done by observation and labour." The Prince had liked his speech; he had said so. And on the morning, when the Prince was leaving, in reply to Jayaji Rao's words, "My State and everything I have is yours," His Royal Highness had answered "I know I have a friend in Scindia." What a splendid reply! Just what was to be expected from the son of the Great Queen across the sea. Those were the very words the Prince had used; again Sir Henry Daly had translated them.

What a pity it was that Sir Henry had retired to England and would return to India no more! But his letters still came from the West, and he still signed himself "your friend and brother" in allusion to the occasion when he and the Maharaja had at one *Sankrant* festival exchanged head dresses and bound the wrist-thread of faternity. Of course, "Daly Sahib" had time and again found fault with things in Gwalior, and he had insisted on the dispersal of the *najib* or police battalions, but he had always been a true friend. Yes, he was Scindia's brother. If only all Englishmen were like Daly Sahib!

But, whether the English were good or bad, they were Scindia's allies by whom he would loyally stand in time of trouble. Wòe to any of the men of Gwalior, if they were untrue to the British, as some had been during the Mutiny! All must be loyal, just as their Ruler was loyal.

At many such a conversation, or rather monologue, for, when unwell, Jayaji Rao would grow moody and, though he talked himself, few dared to converse with him, his son must have sat a silent listener. Thus was loyalty to the British connection indirectly inculcated into his boyish mind. It was bred in the bone too, for in this, as in countless other matters, the mind of the child reflected with astonishing clearness the views of his father.

* * * * * *

It was the summer of 1886. Jayaji Rao's health had now become desparate, and he knew that soon he must die. He would go on pilgrimage to Muttra and Brindaban and so pass away beside the holy Ganges. He reached Bithoor and there fell into a stupor. On the insistence of the Collector of the district he was taken back to Lashkar still unconscious. A few hours later he regained his senses and, at his own request, was moved to Radha Bagh, a little pleasure-house close to the Jai Bilas Palace. There on the 20th of June about eight o'clock in the evening Jayaji Rao's soul left the worn-out casket of his body. His passing was happy. His last words were that he died content, having recovered the Gwalior Fortress and having left a son to succeed him.

The last of three successive Maharajas to be adopted in their youth to the Gwalior *Gadi*, Jayaji Rao was a far abler man than either Doulat Rao or Jankoji Rao. To such a friend as Sir Henry Daly he would complain not without bitterness that he had been neglected in his youth, and that no attention had been paid to his education and training.

In the little boy of eight who had wept most of the time during his interview with Lord Ellenborough after the battle of Maharajpur in 1843, there had been the makings of a big man. From that day during his minority his conduct had been exemplary. If, on the grant of his ruling powers, he had made but little use of his natural gifts, this failure may be largely attributed to a lack of sympathetic guidance during his 'teens. It had needed some such emergency as the Mutiny to bring to the surface his sterling qualities. To judge his rule by the standards of today would be foolish. Admittedly the most capable Maratha Prince of the period, even though he displayed little interest in the civil administration of his State, he at least delivered his domain from internecine feuds. To his son he transmitted with increased force the most admirable of his qualities, so that Madhav Rao Scindia was the better fitted to become the benefactor of those territories which his father had treated as his private property and a source of personal wealth and power.

CHAPTER IV.

1886–1894

THE ashes of Maharaja Jayaji Rao were consigned to the Ganges, a ceremony the final stages of which Rudyard Kipling witnessed and described in *The Pioneer* with all his vivid genius yet with little of his usual sympathy. But the thoughts of the people of Gwalior were not so much centred on the obsequies at Allahabad as on the arrangements which the Government of India had approved for the conduct of affairs in the State during the minority of the nine-year old Maharaja.

The creation of a Council of Regency had been anticipated, but its composition proved a distinct surprise. Surmise had rumoured that with his master's death Khadke, the *Diwan*, would topple from the place of pride that of recent years had been his. To the confusion of the wiseacres he was now found to have been cast for the *rôle* of President in the new Council.

To secure such a position he must, they declared, have bribed a number of important personages! The people of Lashkar were certain that this could have been the only explanation, and by spreading a story to this effect distracted attention from their own failure as political prophets. The real reason of this choice is probably to be found in some wish of the deceased Maharaja who is said to have left it on record—possibly had even addressed the Viceroy on the subject—that Khadke should be nominated to the post. A rumour, false without doubt, but current at the time, averred that the late Ruler had expressed his desire that Dinkar Rao should not be called in to assist the State during the years that must elapse until the young Prince came of age and received his powers. Maybe this rumour was the child of Khadke's own cunning, an unnecessary trick to secure his position against a supposed rival.

In any case it is certain that Dinkar Rao—he was now nearly seventy—had no wish to take a hand once more in the administration of Gwalior. Always a true friend of the State and one who is said to have asked Lord Dufferin to give special thought and attention to the affairs of Gwalior, the ex-*Diwan* recognised that his active work as an administrator was over. He was happier far at Allahabad beside the Ganges, "his thoughts rivetted on the lotus feet of Sri Rama."

The Council of Regency as finally arranged was doubtless a compromise and largely the shrewd work of Sir Lepel Griffin, then the Agent to the Governor-General in Central India. While Khadke was the nominal head, he and all the members had to work "under the advice of the Resident" which euphemism meant nothing less than compliance with the directions of that political officer. It was, moreover, a matter of common knowledge that the colleagues of the "Karbari Sahib" (to give Khadke his usual appellation) were not in all instances the men he would have chosen, had he been allowed a free hand in their selection.

For example, Sahibzada Ghulam Ahmad Khan who, as a revenue officer, had for years served the State with honesty and distinction, could hardly have been *persona gratissima* to Khadke who time and again had tried to remove him from his post in the State.

It was unlikely too that Maratha Sardars of the type of Baba Sahib Sitole and Bapu Sahib Awar, the Commander-in-Chief of Scindia's Army, or his successor, Appa Sahib Angrey, would display undue subserviency to the President of the Council of which they were members now that their official position had risen in importance owing to the death of their late master. Nominated by the Viceroy, as they were, the members of the Council owed nothing to Khadke.

Temak, a near relative of the *Diwan*, was a member, it is true, and so was his protege, Anandi Pershad; but with the work of the Council now closely scrutinised by the Resident, it was impossible for any individual councillor to use his official status for his private ends in so flagrant a manner as had been customary in "the good old days."

The situation may clearly be described thus. Khadke was flattered so far as his dignity went. This Knight-Commander of the Star of India was eventually to receive the unprecedented honour of a salute given him by the British Government, but his powers for extortion and general harm were effectively and instantaneously curtailed. For example, the Judicial Department was protected from all interference by executive officers and no member of the Council had any occasion, indeed much opportunity, for direct influence on the normal course of justice.

With increasing age the ex-Huzuria would appear to have grown more anxious for flattery and outward show, but he was shrewd enough to accept hints or orders from the Agent to the Governor-General or the Resident without question. The courtyard of his house was thronged during the hours of daylight with persons ready, nay anxious, to salaam him, but, with his fortune made, he, until his death in 1888, was content with the elevated divan of President of the Council. In the manifold reforms which were now pressed on the State he took no active part.

To teach the young Maharaja English there was sent from Indore a Kashmiri Brahman, Pundit Dharam Narayan. To this individual's ability and force of character his pupil was much indebted. Of this debt he makes an acknowledgment in the foreword to his "Policy."

To Gwalior too came Surgeon-General, then Major, Crofts as guardian and medical adviser to His Highness. From the start this tall breezy Irishman had more influence over the young Maharaja than any other European, an influence which only terminated with the Surgeon-General's death in 1915.

In addition to this guardian Mr. J. W. D. Johnstone was appointed in 1890 as tutor to superintend the final education of the boy Prince. After the days of his tutorship were over this short-statured but sturdy Scot remained in Gwalior as Inspector-General of State Education until the end of his service in India; and, even after his retirement, "Masterji," to give him the affectionate nickname invented by his pupil, on several occasions revisited the old scene of his labours as His Highness' guest. Though apt to be critical to the last, "Masterji's" originally exiguous temper, which formed the subject of many a local tale, mellowed with age, and in his latter years he was generally regarded with the greatest affection. The old tutor never recovered from the blow caused by the death of his pupil whom he survived by but a few months.

Though it is commonly admitted that the all round influence of the doctor was ever far stronger than that of the schoolmaster, few will deny that both played their parts in developing the great natural powers of the lad committed to their charge.

Fortunate though their selection proved, it is doubtful whether these two educators would have attained much success, had it not been that the boy derived from his parents, and especially his father, a large measure of innate ability and determination. In comparison with the forces of heredity and environment, education can achieve little except possibly by supplying some measure of mental balance and a general sense of proportion.

It would be presumptuous for the non-scientific layman to discuss the obscure question of heredity as exemplified in Madhav Rao Scindia, but at least it is undeniable that the environment of his adolescent years was far from ideal.

His mother's love made her anxious, indeed gave her the intelligence to strive, that her son grow up a good and efficient ruler; but it is more than doubtful if anyone else occupying a position of importance at the palace was genuinely interested in the mental or moral development of the youthful Maharaja.

It was not in any way to the interest of the palace servants at all events that their keen and energetic young master should continue to display keenness and energy throughout his life. Such a catastrophe, as they regarded the matter, would ensure for themselves no easy time in later years. They would have to work with their hands or wits to retain their position, and this, in any case, might be shorn of its privileges. Their whole status would be endangered if their employer took to looking into things for himself. Small would be the chance for any of their number to rise to prominence as an officer courted by the general public. Doubtless the more ambitious of these menials, especially those who could write or read a few words of vernacular, considered that the achievements of Khadke or Temak might be theirs in good time, provided only they could acquire and keep the favour of their master, and that master proved sufficiently complacent. They were too blind to realise that the days were past when any Huzuria might be carrying a minister's commission in his *Kummerbund*.

They had grounds for such optimism. To all outward appearance Khadke was in high favour with the British authorities. All Lashkar was convinced of this. The "Karbari Sahib's" salute gossip attributed to the fact that having forced a confidential servant to reveal the hiding place of much of Jayaji Rao's hoarded wealth, he had loaned the money to the Government of India. Certainly a sum of three and a half crores had been lent on perfectly fair and business-like terms to the Supreme Government, but it is at least open to doubt whether the part played by Khadke in the matter was as dramatic as some alleged. Little credence need be attached to the story that it was only under torture that the confidential servant confessed where the hoard was hidden, and even less to the picturesque tale that on the rendition of the Gwalior Fortress a huge sum had been dug up out of the ground where for nearly thirty years it had been reposing within five feet of the British garrison of the citadel.

To this day rumour avers that, despite the threats of Khadke, one trusted officer of Jayaji Rao, refused to show the whereabouts of the crores in the Moti Mahal of which Khadke later got control and from which he gave the loan.

It is improbable that that officer to whose knowledge of court life at Gwalior during the days of Jayaji Rao much of the information in the preceding pages is due will ever know of this reference to his fidelity; but at least he may herewith fittingly be thanked for his courtesy in supplying information about a period in which without his valuable aid many points would have been wholly obscure.

Ready as Khadke was to accept the new regime and rest on his administrative laurels, his social aspirations soared to giddy heights. Mannu Raja, the daughter of Maharani Lachhmi Bai and so half-sister to the young Maharaja, was as yet unwed. Khadke considered she would be a suitable match for his son! His ambitions leaped even higher. On several occasions in the past history of Gwalior the Ruler of the time had married his chief minister's daughter. Khadke had no daughter available as a bride for his youthful master; but he had a grand-daughter! Were she affianced to the boy Maharaja, the Khadke family could never be despised in future.

For such a consummation he intrigued quietly: but he had set his aim too high. Both the surviving Maharanis, Lachhmi Bai and "Jija Maharaj," opposed the suggestion firmly. So did the big Maratha Sardars who threatened to debar Khadke from entrance to the palace on any pretext whatever. In the face of such opposition he was forced to drop the scheme at the last moment.

He is said never to have recovered from this blow to his self-esteem. Half-heartedly he plotted for the removal of "Jija Maharaj" and her son from Lashkar to Ujjain, but his failure to degrade the Scindia stock by an intermarriage with a family which is not recognised as true-born Maratha was a crushing defeat to his pride. His visits to the palace almost ceased; he is reported to have feared physical violence there.

He had not long to live. To quote the opening words of the first Gwalior Administration Report ever published "The State suffered a severe loss by the untimely death of Rao Raja Sir Ganpat Rao Khadke, Shumsher Jung Bahadur, K. C. S. I., on the 17th August 1888."

His place was taken by Sardar Krishna Rao Jadho, commonly known as "Bapu Sahib," maternal grandfather of the boy Maharaja, whose mother was at the same time nominated as "Regent" for the remaining period of her son's minority. This title conferred no administrative powers on the Maharani, but at least it gave her a greater voice than before in matters concerning the personal comfort and general upbringing of her son.

The Administration Report to which reference has just been made deals with a period from August 1888 to June 1892 and is an informative document both from its contents and its manifest omissions.

The first and longest chapter deals with Police. It records serious religious riots between Hindus and Mohammedans at Ujjain where the Dasehra and Moharram festivals both fell on the same date and several lives were lost. In later years the same coincidence of dates occurred. On the second occasion a quarter of a century afterwards there was no such catastrophe. With Madhav Rao Scindia actively participating in both Dasehra and Moharram, Hindus and Mohammedans alike on the same day attended each other's religious celebrations at Lashkar, and nowhere in the whole State was there aught but complete harmony.

A lengthy portion of the first chapter deals with dacoity and violent crimes. In spite of the Army reinforcing the Police, the bandits seem to have been more than a match for the forces of law and order. At this time a large proportion of the Rajputs in the State were at least passively disloyal and certainly gave no active help in the apprehension of cattle-lifters, highway-robbers, and house-breakers, most of whom were their own caste fellows.

Perhaps things were really better than they had been under Khadke, during the last year of whose regime there had admittedly been 3,863 persons wanted as dacoits apart from highway robbers and cattle-lifters!

The Police uniforms were not in proper condition and the constabulary had no rifles such as the dacoits possessed. They had to risk their lives in catching such criminals for five rupees a month! In the circumstances it is at least arguable that economic reasons as much as lack of courage made the Police ready to stand in with, rather than up to, the gangs of dacoits.

The second chapter of the Administration Report headed "Judicial" is of some interest since it shows that the reign of law had as yet hardly commenced in Gwalior. A few excerpts may be given as illustrative of the embryonic state of justice at the time. Section (*j*) reads "According to circular order No. 36, dated 15th April 1877, no transfer of property by sale or gifts was to be considered valid if made by a person during his illness preceding his death. On the contrary, it was valid that properties thus transferred should be forfeited to the State."

This order, conflicting as much with the precepts of Hindu or Mohammedan Law as with the principles of equity, was repealed.

Section (*k*) "Formerly there was no provision for the payment of the cost of feeding under trial prisoners in the District and Pargana lock-ups."

It was now arranged that such persons should at least be given food, if on no extravagant scale, to judge by the provision made for feeding prisoners at the central jail, where the allowance per prisoner was raised about this time from three half-pence to a penny three-farthings a day!

Section (*n*) "Under the law formerly in force, prisoners sentenced to imprisonment for a term less than six months were not provided with cloths (*sic*) by the State. In consequence of this they were forced to undergo the rigor of the cold climate which disabled them to perform hard labour."

By a merciful innovation all prisoners now received prison garb without regard to their terms of imprisonment.

Section (*r*) "There were no rules regarding the trial of civil and criminal cases in which Ekkande, Hoozooriat Paigah and Paigahnaweas were parties."

By a new circular such persons who come under the general head of palace guards were at least not entirely exempted from the operations of the law courts.

Section (*p*)..."fines inflicted as part of punishment used to be recovered from such prisoners as were unable to pay them and had undergone imprisonment in default after the release of the prisoners."

This oppressive regulation was cancelled.

The same chapter records the fact that there were no rules regarding cases to do with forged documents, false evidence, and the institution of false claims, nor relating to the arrest of prisoners accused of criminal offences if in the service of Sardars, Darakhdars and Mankaris. Instances might be multiplied from the pages of this Administration Report to show that the ideas of law and justice, let alone those of equity, were hardly comprehended by the people of Gwalior as a whole, but the extracts given above are more than enough to prove this point which, if of no great interest, cannot pass unnoticed.

Chapter III—Revenue—begins:—"This Department is presided over by Santoji Rao Temak, Member of the Council of Regency. He is one of the oldest and most experienced Officers and has served in various Departments of the State." He was assisted by a *Naib-Diwan*, also "an old and able servant of the State."

Reform in the Revenue Department was no easy task. The "good old days" were not to be allowed to pass in a moment; but at least Sir Michael Filose was *Sar Suba* in Malwa where he was carrying out a settlement and modifying the excessive demands formerly made on the cultivators in that province.

In Northern Gwalior too a revenue survey had been forced on the Council, though this settlement, the work of several persons, was not above criticism and later needed much revision. Colonel D. G. Pitcher, Deputy Commissioner of Hardoi, was imported to build up a Land Records Department and train the *Patwaris* or village accountants. He gave many useful years of service to the State and ever retained the regard of the Ruler of Gwalior.

Retiring in 1903, the Colonel, some twenty years later, revisited Gwalior as a guest of the State and showed that, despite his eighty-five years, his faculties were as acute as ever. He receives grateful recognition in the foreword to "The General Darbar Policy" as the man who gave its author, Madhav Rao Scindia, his final training in survey and settlement work.

The Administration Report of 1888-92 speaks of a new branch of the Revenue Department, namely, that of Irrigation. This Department, which in subsequent years has attained much importance and needs further extension had not existed during the times of Jayaji Rao. A few large reservoirs in the neighbourhood of Lashkar had been constructed by Sir Michael Filose, but these tanks had been designed chiefly for watering the palace grounds and not for general agricultural purposes.

The naive summary of the advantage of this young Irrigation Department, the barely concealed apology for its creation, attempts little more than a demonstration of a probable increase in the land revenue by this means. The Council at least had not those bowels of compassion for the lot of the *ryot* which the young Maharaja of Gwalior on attaining his powers so amply displayed.

The Postal Department, another branch of the revenue, was (to quote the report) "presided by (*sic*) Pundit Sheo Charan who is an able and intelligent officer." He will come up for unpleasant notice later; but meanwhile it is worth recording that a revised Postal Convention between the Government of India and Gwalior was concluded in 1888.

A section, No. 110, of the Report, though comprising but two lines of print is worthy of mention. It runs:—"Some of the State Postal runners while on duty had encounters with and captured dacoits. In order to encourage them I (*i.e.*, the President of the Council) sanctioned suitable rewards for them."

A census in 1891, the second taken in the State, showed that the population was some three million three hundred thousand odd souls as compared with just under three million in 1881, but it is more than doubtful if the first numbering of the people had been at all accurate. Even the figures for 1891 are distinctly suspect. In any case the decade 1881-1891 had shown a serious reduction in the number of inhabited villages.

Chapter IV deals with the Public Works Department, also a new creation. Presided over by Anandi Pershad and after his death by Bhaiya Balwant Rao Scindia it enjoyed the assistance of a Mr. Harris, a lent Officer and a very able engineer. To Mr. Harris are due not only several roads—for the pressing need of communications brooked no further delay—but also the finest of the modern buildings erected at the capital, among them the Jayaji Memorial Hospital and the Victoria College.

Mr. Harris was evidently a hustler, for the Report records that in two financial years, in the period from August 1888 to June 1892, he exceeded his budgetted allotments. Evidently this was no very great offence in those days, though a red paper slip bound into the main body of the Report as an after-thought adds that such excess of expenditure in future must receive the Council's previous sanction. After all until this Council of Regency came into being, the State had never dreamed of any regular budget or financial rules,

In Bhaiya Balwant Rao Mr. Harris had a chief well able to appreciate architectural excellencies and possibly one who made no demur to the engineer's proposal to build a palace at Ujjain, a work which for all its artistic merit was no suitable project for a minority administration.

The next chapter deals with Scindia's Army and records the acceptance by the Supreme Government of the offer from the Darbar of two regiments of Imperial Service Cavalry and a Transport Corps.

The failing health of Jayaji Rao's later years accounted in part no doubt for the diminished attention paid to the army as compared with the two decades immediately following the Mutiny. Even the so-called regular troops would in 1886 seem to have been in a parlous condition so far as equipment went. At this time they were certainly quite unfit for active duties away from their headquarters and admittedly (to quote the report) heavily in debt to certain bankers who had advanced loans at exorbitant rates of interest.

Better times, however, were in store for Scindia's Army which at least had the great traditions of De Boigne's brigades behind it; but little real improvement could result until their young leader grew old enough to knock into shape his cavalry and infantry and, with his personal enthusiasm to back up the efforts of his own officers and those lent from the Indian Army, forge units which at least were worthy to play a part in many theatres of war during the great struggle of 1914-19.

The Educational Department—their activities under the guidance of Sahibzada Ghulam Ahmad are recorded in Chapter VI of the Report—had by 1892 succeeded in getting an annual grant of a little over a lakh of rupees. In four years the number of students had about doubled. For a State of over three million persons and roughly ten thousand villages there were after the Council had been in existence for nearly six years, only 175 schools of all grades and very few indeed in any villages; but, for all such latter-day criticism, the Member in charge of Education had succeeded in getting the budget at least quadrupled. Considering its resources, Gwalior might still be the most backward of the larger Native States in the provision of academic instruction, but Education had come to stay.

The remaining chapters of the Administration Report record the establishment at the capital of a municipality, no democratic institution indeed, but a semi-official department. Spasmodic attempts were made to widen some of the narrow streets and even a few drains were being constructed, though little money was expended on general sanitation.

The Report too describes the procedure adopted by the President of the Council in his correspondence with the Residency and tells of the sanction given for two broad-gauge lines, the Goona-Bina and Ujjain-Bhopal sections, a total of 185 miles to be constructed from the State funds. A noteworthy item records that Surgeon-Major Crofts not content with his dual post of Medical Adviser to the Maharaja and Residency Surgeon had taken charge of the development of a State Medical Department. The Report proper ends with a description of the President's own tours in the districts, excursions in which *shikar* was at all times a prominent feature. An out-and-out Indian nobleman, Sardar Bapu Sahib Jadho appears to have discovered all to be well with the State of Gwalior!

As appendices to the Report are attached detailed descriptions of the wedding of Mannu Raja, His Highness' half-sister, of His Highness' own marriage, of a visit to Gwalior of the late ill-starred Czar, then Heir-Apparent to the throne of all the Russias, and of a viceregal visit, by Lord Lansdowne.

It is evident that Sardar Jadho Sahib much appreciated the importance derived from his office on such ceremonial occasions. That office had come to him by virtue of his relationship: he could not have claimed it on grounds of superior talent, nor kept it for long, had times been different. His personality inspired Sir Lepel Griffin who some time before had retired from Central India, to frame a classic phrase which still adorns an old issue of the *Asiatic Quarterly Review.*

Apt and pithy as it may be, it errs from good taste, and the reader's curiosity will not be satisfied by its repetition here.

Sardar Bapu Sahib Jadho was true to type. He had been brought up as a nobleman. In early youth the development of a strong frame and equitation had received attention; later marksmanship and an appreciation of music. So he grew up to be an excellent shot and a patron of indoor sport, bird fights being his chief delight.

He had polished manners and much suavity of disposition, but the performance of public business had had no place in the programme of his instruction. Whether from this initial handicap or owing to his conception of the dignity of clothing a nobleman, for the transaction of the duties of his Office the attendance and indeed the advice of "*Peshkars*" were indispensable, even in matters of elementary routine.

He never allowed himself to be overweighted by the cares of State. Official business was not permitted to trench upon his predilection; it came in for its share of attention by being fitted into the most convenient hour of the day, generally four in the afternoon, though the constant realisation that some urgent request or hint might have come from the Residency requiring his immediate and unqualified assent, tended at times to make his start at his work a rather flurried one.

But if not brilliant, Bapu Sahib Jadho was at least kind-hearted. Born of good family, he did not disgrace his position by corrupt methods such had been the daily habit of his predecessor. It was probably not to the disadvantage of Gwalior that so complaisant and easy-going a Sardar was just then President of the Council of Regency. If the State was to be cured of its general demoralisation, it was as well that the first steps of treatment should not be too hurried. An abler leech would soon take up the task and one moreover gifted in the eyes of his subjects, with divine right to administer the cure, however drastic or unnecessary they might consider the remedy to be.

In the meantime Madhav Rao Scindia in spite of his youth was already keeping a shrewd eye on affairs and making mental notes which were to be of service to him during the whole of his life as a Ruler. He was giving himself at least as much education as he was receiving from his tutor or his medical adviser. It had never been expected that he would be a book-worm or indeed particularly studious; such was not the custom of Maratha Princes in their youth. But it was a genuine surprise to all that his bent turned so much to practical matters. Who could have anticipated that a Maharaja of Gwalior would devote his spare time to the smithy and the carpenter's bench? The practice of such crafts was not forced upon him by his tutors; of his own accord he applied his hands and mind to them, thereby giving himself unconsciously a course of manual training that was of infinite value to his general mental development.

For it was manual rather than technical training that he gave himself. As it has been well said in pointing out the difference "the first box a boy makes is an education to its maker, the second and third are but matters of habit." Unwittingly the boy Prince worked on this plan. While always active, he was ever engaged on some novelty. One day it would be the making of a boat, the next some chemical experiment and the manufacturing of fireworks which possibly exploded sooner than he intended. The third day might witness a new-born interest in mechanics, centring perhaps in a model steam-engine which with an over-sized boiler fitted to it would be found to work at a rate never contemplated by its designer. On the fourth day, after lessons in language were over, electricity might be the occupation chosen, and a variety of dignified personages subjected to galvanic shocks.

This Ruler in the making was not prepared to waste all his spare time in sitting still and listening to the flattery of his attendants. He was always doing something and keeping his retinue extremely busy. They had to join him and put their shoulders to the wheel. If the task of the moment was that of emptying out some reservoir and collecting the fish from the bottom of the tank, they too like their master had to wade in the mud and work. Or if he were cooking, a favourite pastime, they had to collect sticks, light a fire, and get the smoke in their eyes, while feigning an interest in a pursuit which they abhorred. Even then the chances were that their pretended absorption would be detected and that they would be punished for their hypocrisy by some practical joke.

From an early age Madhav Rao Scindia had been taught to ride and shoot. He had now to supplement these accomplishments, according to the old Persian tradition of royal education. All that he gained from books, all that he learned by experience had to be put to practical use. For example, when learning military drill he was not content with gaining for himself a practical knowledge of a soldier's duties. As he says in his "Policy" he learned to express himself simply, yet forcibly, and acquired the art of public speaking by lecturing to the recruits with the sole object of giving vent to his ideas in clear and intelligible language. To quote his own words: "I also used to question the men as to what they had understood. If they failed to explain a point correctly, I concluded that it was due to my faulty expressions and then I tried to correct myself."

Although he lacked inches and the ideal build for a horseman, he had quickly become a strong and easy rider, who in later life could cover long distances and still be able to do a heavy day's work after his journey.

In giving his views on equestrian skill he enjoins that "at least so much practice in riding should be attained that at least three or four horses one may be able to tire without tiring oneself, and be able to ride 50 or 60 miles and then be able to attend to one's work without feeling fatigued."

From a very early age he had shown promise of becoming an excellent shot, not merely at a target, but at big or small game. Bapu Sahib Jadho, his grandfather, was always willing to take him out for a day in the jungle but, being a jealous shot, never gave his grandson an opportunity to shoot the tiger or other animal which was being driven towards the guns. Such expeditions became a wearisome business to the high-mettled youth and at last, greatly daring, he shot dead the tiger which was being driven up to his grandsire's *Machchan.* Bapu Sahib is alleged to have been "furious" but, as His late Highness often said when telling the story, he appeased the old man's wrath and from that day, whether in *shikar* or in any other business, he always did what he liked with him!

Meanwhile at his books the Prince learned two vernaculars, Marathi and Urdu, both rather imperfectly, English moderately well, though the spelling was always his master, a little Arithmetic, a certain amount of Geography and more thoroughly Map-making and Map-reading, also some History, both Indian and English, though he found little interest in the last subject. It is unfortunate that he received no instruction in Economics, a most necessary discipline for one born to the position of an autocrat and to the command of large resources. The accepted elementary laws of political economy would seem to come to none, even the most talented, by intuition; they are only acquired by serious study and a painful grounding.

While usually shrewd in actual matters of business the late Maharaja had not the grasp of public finance that would have been his, if he had been taught in youth the first principles of economics.

Had he been fortunate enough to receive some training in the science of finance, he might have saved himself many weary hours in later life when going through every single item in the budget of each State department!

For this omission it is difficult to blame any of his tutors. The time at their disposal was very limited. Their pupil, though still a minor, was expected to attend a variety of religious and social ceremonies; his education was seriously interrupted at one time by an attack of enteric; it was common knowledge that he would get his powers at eighteen and before that time he had to learn the elements of law and administration generally; it was essential that he should receive military, judicial, and revenue training and, to crown all difficulties, it was certain that during his hours of leisure away from his teachers the environment into which he would naturally fall would not be of the best. Heredity and custom were pulling one way, formal education with less force the other. It was only his passion for being busy, for doing something, and especially working with his hands, which prevented his development from proving catastrophic.

In January 1891 a few months after the completion of his fourteenth year he was married. It would be interesting to reproduce *in extenso* the whole six pages of the official report of the ceremonies as prepared by Sardar Jadho, but space forbids. Some extracts, however, cannot be omitted.

"As the time of His Highness the Maharaja's attaining his majority was fast approaching, Her Highness the Regent and myself thought it incumbent to propose to celebrate his marriage in the month of January 1891 with the beautiful daughter of Madho Rao *alias* Bhau Sahib Mohite belonging to a respectable family at Satara."

Such is Jadho Sahib's opening. He continues: "I took a deep interest in making arrangements for the celebration of the marriage. An estimate of rupees twenty-two lacs was sanctioned by the Council for this purpose in the beginning of December 1890.

"Many grand Darbars attended with dancing and music and special feasts were held in the city.

"The population of the whole city from a Sardar to a poor man gaily decorated their houses with parti-colored banners as a mark of rejoicing.

"Such Darbars were also held in all the chief towns in the State and a large amount of money was distributed in charity.

"Effective triumphal arches were erected on the following main roads (enumeration unnecessary) and *Nakkar-khanas* were posted thereon (the arches) which with their joyous sounds enlivened the public.

"Although there are numerous lofty and spacious palaces, belonging to the State, in the city, yet pursuant to the time-honoured custom, some *Mandaps* and *Pandals* (marquees and tents) were erected and properly decorated at a cost of Rs. 68,352.

"One of these *Mandaps* was erected in the Moti Mahal quadrangle. It was 100 feet long and 82 broad and consisted of a central Hall with raised dias (*sic*) embellished with gold and silver embroidered cloth and tassels and two side aisles."

This marquee was utilised for the first of the ceremonies on the 29th of December. A largely attended Darbar was held, "Dancing of Nautch girls commenced first at 5 P. M. The President and a few Sardars proceeded to the temporary residence of the bride's father and the *Haldi* ceremony having been observed according to custom, the band playing at intervals, they returned to the Moti Mahal at about 8 P.M.

"Subsequently Madho Rao *alias* Bhau Sahib Mohite, accompanied by his relatives, dependants, and some Sardars, proceeded to the Moti Mahal where the *Haldi* ceremony was observed to the bride-groom at an auspicious hour, followed by the firing of 21 guns to announce the public joyous event. The band played and the drums and trumpets were perpetually being sounded."

"At 8-45 P. M. His Highness came to the Darbar and the whole assembly paid their respect to Him (the H is the printer's) according to their ranks."

The next day saw the distribution of saffron-coloured dresses of honour to the Sardars and officers of the State. The last day of the year was occupied by the *Garagner* ceremonies held in the Zenana.

The New Year started with the *Shrimanti* ceremonies. "For this purpose special *Mandaps* were erected in the *Dasehra* plain...which were richly decorated with flags, banners, flower-pots and seemed almost like a pleasure garden. It was supported on iron posts decorated with gold and silver lace and flowers. A beautiful raised *Singhasan* or *Dias* (*sic*) fitted with *panes* (why the italics) of glass for His Highness was placed in the centre of *Mandap*. Dancing and music were going on in the *Mandap*."

There is an account of another *Mandap* for His Highness' mother and step-mother and of a *Shamiana* "occupied by the sacred image of *Shri Gopalji Maharaja*, the titulary diety (*sic*) of the Maharaja,...where according to the usual custom the learned *Shastris* commenced to recite portions of the Hindu Scripture or *Vedas*.

"Dancing and music were going on, artillery salutes, and a *fieu-de-joi (sic)* were fired. The band played the National Anthem. Alms were distributed liberally to the poor, due *Dakshanas* with turbans and pairs of shawls were given to the forty Pundits who officiated at the ceremony and to many others according to their merits"...

"The State drums were beaten and fireworks were let off on a large scale."

Such were merely some of the preliminaries: the actual marriage ceremonies did not take place until the next day, January 2.

Then "the marriage procession was formed in a right royal way and left Moti Mahal for the big *Mandap* in the Kampu-Kothi. This *Mandap*...had three wooden arches gaily decorated with splendid ponaromas *(sic)* and prizes of red...such a big *Mandap* was never before erected in Lashkar." It still probably holds the record.

"His Highness having put on a bridal chaplet and lots of jewelry mounted on a caparisoned elephant and started at the head of a procession which was formed of all the Sardars, Members of Council," etc. It ended with "other respectable citizens and well-wishers of the State."

More illuminations, more fireworks, more *fieu-de-jois* and more band playing.

The marriage "took place in full pomp and splendour just at 5-4 P. M., the auspicious moment decided upon by the Astrologers."

More salutes of artillery, more "*fieu*," etc., again the National Anthem, more fireworks "and the scene was very imposing."

"The Resident at Gwalior accompanied by some European Ladies and Gentlemen arrived in the nick of time and like the other assembly threw *Akshat* at the happy married couple and congratulated His Highness and the President on behalf of the British Government."

The evening ended with certain ceremonies behind the *purdah* when "Her Highness the Regent put round a necklace of valuable pearls on the bride's neck."

The next three days were each marked by further ceremonies but of a quieter nature. The 6th of January saw the resumption of illuminations, fireworks, a caparisoned elephant as a mode of conveyance, salvos of artillery, salutes, "*fieu*," etc. On that day "a new name, Chinkoo Raja," was given to the bride.

The 7th seems to have been a quiet day. The 8th saw another Darbar at the Moti Mahal. The 9th was free from ceremony, the 10th was devoted to alms-giving. The 11th saw yet another Darbar at the Moti Mahal; when dancing began at 9 A. M., and dinner was taken at 1 P. M. Except for minor ceremonies on the 22nd and a dinner given on the 24th, the wedding was complete.

The fourteen-year old bridegroom had been well and truly married. To judge from his innate aversion to undue pomp and show, a genuine sentiment which he continually displayed throughout his life, it is doubtful if he had enjoyed the display nearly as much as had his grandfather, the organiser of the ceremonies.

The Resident at Gwalior who had arrived at the wedding "in the nick of time" was Colonel, later Sir David Barr, for whom the young Maharaja had conceived an affection which lasted until the death of that famous officer.

The help that Sir David Barr consistently gave His Highness receives acknowledgment in the foreword to the "Policy."

As Resident at Gwalior, as Agent to the Governor-General in Central India or at Hyderabad, and lastly as a Member of the Secretary of State for India's Council, Sir David Barr, by his advice and active aid to a Ruler for whom from the first he had had a genuine regard, rendered services of great value to the Gwalior State.

At the end of 1891 His Highness got his first sight of the Indian Army. The newly formed Gwalior Imperial Service Cavalry had been invited to attend a camp of exercise at Aligarh and the young Prince had received an invitation from Sir Frederick, later Lord, Roberts, then Commander-in-Chief in India, to be present for part of the manœuvres. The friendship thus formed lasted without intermission until the great Field-Marshal's death in France. It is doubtful, however, if "Bobs" at his first meeting could have guessed that the boy Maharaja would ever develop into a keen and instinctive soldier. His Highness on his visit to Meerut which had been chosen as his headquarters during the manœuvres, was accompanied, not only by his medical adviser and tutor, but also by his mother and his girl wife, as well as by a large and not entirely military-looking retinue.

Since his father's death Madhav Rao Scindia had so far seldom left the confines of his State. The ten days' outing which he now enjoyed must have been done much to create in him an interest in civil as well as military matters. He was only just fifteen, but he was quick enough to notice not merely the leeway which the Gwalior Regiments had to make up; he saw too that even at manœuvres a large band of servants detailed for his personal attendance made him unduly conspicuous. After the first day all except one or two soldiers had to remain behind at headquarters, and then he was able to enjoy himself and learn things. The boy was growing up. On his return he gave his views to the commander of his army. The Imperial Service troops from Gwalior had done fairly well and received a cash reward, but they must do much better, and the general level of efficiency of the regular and irregular troops must be raised as soon as possible.

Yet it was impossible for the boy to devote as much time to the army as he wished. There were too many demands on his time. His general education had to continue, and as it was practically certain that within three years he would get his ruling powers, there were various subjects, such as law and general administration, in which he would require training. It was necessary too to tour about in his State to see matters for himself at first hand. There were as well his mechanical hobbies in which his interest never flagged.

For the moment his interest was centred on steam locomotives. At his request his tutor, while on leave, had ordered a miniature two-foot gauge engine and some half a mile of track. The rails were laid in the palace grounds, which still were divided into several sections by high walls. The laying of the track necessitated the dismantling of several of these walls and their material served conveniently as ballast for the permanent way. The toy train made its trial trip, but half a mile of line was far too short. Almost by the time the engine had gathered speed, it was necessary to close the throttle to avoid running into the dead end. So two miles more of track were called for, but the laying of this meant an extension of the line outside the palace grounds towards Morar.

A railway system was springing up, and railways could not be constructed without the sanction of the Government of India! Explanations had to be offered, and as finally arranged the line was extended to Sussera, a shooting box some seven or eight miles from the capital.

From this genesis sprang the Gwalior Light Railway, some two hundred and fifty miles in length, which today yields a fair dividend on the capital invested and has in famine time proved of incalculable benefit in carrying supplies of food to the more remote tracts in Northern Gwalior and especially to Sheopur.

That the gauge of this railway is still two foot instead of two foot six which might have proved a more economic one and that the alignment of the Bhind section does not follow the best traffic route is due to the fact that His late Highness in building a commercial light railway thought fit to utilise the portion already constructed to Sussera.

It was characteristic of him that he would never, if possible, scrap anything which was already in existence but utilise it in some extension of an old scheme or as part of a new one. This trait, illustrative of his innately practical mind, apparently made for economy and occasionally secured other advantages as well; but on the whole it operated to effect schemes, whatever they were, less satisfactorily than their authors could have wished.

An anecdote may be given of the day when the boy Maharaja from the engine's footplate drove his train to within two miles of Sussera. The line had not yet been laid right up to the shooting box. The object of the expedition was buck shooting. Sardar Jadho, needless to say, was of the party. A day's *shikar* always appealed to him far more than his official files.

Madhav Rao Scindia was stalking a black buck. It was a good head, but wary, and uneasily it moved away. The young *shikari* followed it. It came in the direction of Jadho Sahib, who fired and dropped it. The grand-son was furious with his grand-father. He sulked and refused his midday repast. He would not accept the excuses of his elderly relative. He would not even eat his supper. In vain various persons tried to persuade him. They only encouraged his obstinacy.

Strategy was the only thing. Jadho Sahib, under advice, feigned a sudden and serious illness. It was sunstroke. The doctors did not know if he would recover. "The Sardar Sahib" could hardly live unless he took their medicines, but the patient would take nothing, neither food nor drugs, until his grand-son had eaten.

The news came to the boy. He rushed to the old man's side. His patient's eyes were closed. He was obviously very ill but could just murmur that he would swallow his dose, if his Maharaja ate his food. Sitting by the bedside, Madhav Rao Scindia took his meal, and, still lying in the bed, Jadho Sahib his medicine. The recovery was very rapid and, the story goes, that grand-sire and grand-son made a late night of it. However, Jadho Sahib could not play such a trick twice. Perhaps he felt that he had asserted himself sufficiently.

Possibly the late Maharaja had in his mind his grand-father's jealousy as a shot when early on in his "Policy" he penned the lines "Similarly, when going out shooting, the tutors ignore their duty and desire to have a first shot in precedence of the Prince. As a matter of fact, it is their duty to train the Prince in the art of shooting."

Yet he had no reason to complain of his own training in *shikar*. By the age of sixteen he was an exceptionally good shot either with gun or rifle.

Sussera with its herds of buck was not only used as a pleasure resort. An old house there was turned into the model of a *Subat*, or collector's office, and in it the boy learned the details of survey and settlement work. Under Colonel Pitcher's instruction he acquired from the bottom upwards a knowledge of the duties of *Patwari*, *Qanungo*, *Naib-Tehsildar*, *Tehsildar*, and *Suba* and quickly showed that he had grasped the main principles of land revenue work. From the first his intellect displayed a meticulous attention to detail. Various boys, the sons of Maratha gentlefolk, who had read with him in the two classes which Mr. Johnstone had formed for the general education of his pupil, were now unmistakably proved his mental inferiors. They had not his aptitude to turn their minds to new subjects, nor the capacity to keep up with the adaptable brain of their future Ruler. They might be of use where purely physical qualities were required, but they had not the responsiveness, nor the intellectual pliancy of the boy Maharaja.

His Highness about this time began to make short tours to the various districts of the State, and the menials who accompanied his camp soon found that such tours were not the peculatory progresses of the olden time. The number of personal attendants was rigidly curtailed and they had to work hard while on tour. They got little chance of extorting money from the *ryots* for their young master was watching them too closely. He was ready to receive a petition from any one, high or low, to look into it himself, and to deal with it on the spot. His servants probably consoled themselves with the idea that such energy on the part of their lord could not last. It was all very well while the boy was still being trained; no doubt he had to win the favourable regard of the Resident, but, once he got his powers, he naturally would cease to work, and the palace menials would have their chance once more.

It may have been a comforting thought; it certainly was a false optimism. The "good old days" had gone never to return.

The Maharaja was in his eighteenth year. Soon he would get his powers. He was already being taught the elements of judicial work, a subject in which Colonel, later Sir, Donald Robertson, the sympathetic Resident of the time, was taking much interest. The ballroom at the Jai Bilas Palace was turned into the model of a court in which Madhav Rao Scindia sat recording evidence in cases that came before him. With him was a qualified judge to see what decision the lad arrived at, a decision which would only be the verdict of the court, provided it was strictly in accord with the laws of evidence and the provisions of the Gwalior Criminal or Civil Code as the case might be.

The Resident was a constant, indeed a most welcome, visitor, for the relations between the Maharaja and this Political Officer had been most cordial from their first meeting.

In connection with this training in law His late Highness often told a story which may be cited here.

The day was hot, the case a dull one, dealing perhaps with some trivial civil claim. The young Maharaja (it is his own confession) had had a late night. The Resident was paying one of his usual visits to the ballroom court, but it was monotonous work recording tiresome evidence when the recorder's head was tired. His eyes closed, his head rested on the desk. Madhav Rao Scindia was asleep.

Silently at a signal from the Resident the court emptied; judge, plaintiff, and defendant, and the general public crept away. The boy slept on peacefully.

After a while he awoke with a start. In an instant he recalled what had happened. Beneath his hand lay the note-book in which he had been taking down the evidence. The record had come to a sudden stop in the middle of a sentence. He hurried off to the Residency and apologised to Colonel Robertson. The Political Officer was no man to feel that he had been slighted by a lad's lapse into dreamland. Smilingly he accepted the apology.

There is no other recorded instance of Madhav Rao Scindia, as boy or man, falling asleep over his office work. For the rest of his life it may be said that he was wide-awake even when asleep. Physically he certainly was; such was the formation of his attractive and prominent eyes which were never completely closed even when he was in deep slumber.

The Council of Regency continued its work. Now that certain reforms had been started and such State departments as the Land Records and Settlement or the P. W. D. were in efficient hands, pressure from the Residency seems to have slackened somewhat. To judge from the reports submitted one year after another by certain subordinate departments to the Council, the Members of that body would seem to have seized the opportunity of this relief to take life easy.

For example, the Chief Justice year after year requests that the civil and criminal laws of the State should be revised and codified instead of resting on a number of circulars often of a contradictory nature. He tells too of the construction of a new gaol at Sabalgarh which cannot be used as he can get no replies to his frequent demands for some warders to watch the prisoners. The administration of justice seems to have been improving, however, and the work connected with the appeals from decisions of the Chief Court executed with despatch and general approval by Sahibzada Ghulam Ahmad.

Dacoity again, though still distressingly common, was yet not quite so much of an everyday occurrence as in the past. Colonel Pitcher, whose surveyors were on occasion threatened with personal violence by these bandits, remarks that his statistics showed no relation between dacoity and any overassessment of land revenue.

The *Subas* and other district revenue officers seem to have spent little time in touring. They stayed close to headquarters and in a most suspicious manner refused to consider a proposal of the postal department for making possible the payment of land revenue by money order.

With increasing age the Members of the Council toured less than formerly and, greatly to the benefit of Malwa, Sir Michael Filose was left to administer that province much as he thought fit. Sardar Bapu Sahib Jadho appears to have stuck to Lashkar and no longer traversed the districts to find all, not only the *shikar*, good.

The time was drawing near when the young Maharaja would get his powers. He was already in charge of one department, that of the palace household, and displaying an awkward attention to detail, and checking time-honoured waste and abuses generally.

There was considerable discussion in Lashkar and elsewhere as to whom he would appoint as his *Diwan*. Of course, new brooms swept clean, and his energy and assiduity were most commendable but it was not the Maratha tradition that the Maharaja of Gwalior should pay much, if any, attention to administration.

The last year of the Council of Regency dragged on. Early in its course the Maharaja paid a short visit to Calcutta to say farewell to Lord Lansdowne, the retiring Viceroy. He also spent a week's holiday in Agra. Except for these two outings he remained in Gwalior paying the closest attention to the department in his charge and learning the elements of general administration.

On December 15, 1894, when he was some two months past his eighteenth birthday, Madhav Rao Scindia was invested with full powers by Lord Elgin, the new Viceroy, through his Agent, Sir David Barr. The final words of that Political Officer's address to the Maharaja on this occasion may be quoted:

"On this auspicious day, when Your Highness' minority ends, and you enter upon your duties as a Ruler, I would ask you to resolve so to rule your actions that you may uphold the dignity and honour of your name and secure the peace, prosperity, and happiness of your State and your people."

With such advice from his old friend Madhav Rao Scindia took possession of his heritage. That his heritage was so goodly was due largely to the work done forty years earlier by an old man who had attended the Investiture Darbar. Sir Dinkar Rao had for this great occasion paid his last visit to Gwalior. Supremely happy he returned to Allahabad where, full of years and honour, he soon passed away.

CHAPTER V.

1895–1903

AMONG the thirty or more rulers of the bigger Indian States the proportion of princes who could be found ready to say from the heart that they were really happy men must be indeed very small. It is no fortunate fate to be born or adopted to the *gadi* of one of these principalities. To succeed to almost absolute powers, to a personal autocracy that is nowadays protected, not even tempered by assassination, may, according to Hindu ideas, be an individual's *karma*, but it is certainly his curse.

And this question of happiness would seem to have little or nothing to do with another, namely, to what extent Indian princes may or may not feel their responsibility towards the subjects over whom their will is for all practical purposes supreme. So long as a Maharaja is a despot, even a benevolent despot, he does not appear to get any satisfaction from his good actions, at all events during his life-time. In other words, in his case virtue does not seem to be its own reward; it brings with it little satisfaction.

For any Indian prince to have a sense of balance, of mental proportion, must be an extremely difficult matter; for, however much he gathers out of books or from society at large, he gets but little chance of education by experience.

The most valuable everyday lessons that a commoner learns or teaches himself come not from the printed page, but from the pursuit by his own exertions of money, power, and sex; and success in the pursuit of these three things, whether they be mere delusions or givers of real happiness, affords no satisfaction unless they be attained by personal effort.

Yet to a Chief who, once his schooldays are over, is within his own State amenable of necessity to no one, to nothing, not even to public opinion, since that corrective has as yet hardly developed among his subjects, the attainment of the three above-cited blessings or curses comes without the need for personal exertion.

Without the effective mental check which self-administered education can give, any Maharaja must be more at the mercy of heredity and environment than the meanest of his subjects.

Whatever may be the truth of this analysis Madhav Rao Scindia, on taking up the reins of Government in Gwalior, was a happy man. If in the years to come happiness degenerated into optimism and optimism then yielded to sadness, the tragedy in his case is somewhat lightened by the reflection that to the last the loyalty and affection of his people were genuine sentiments which had been inspired in them solely by his fascinating personality and his unceasing labours on their behalf. If such were the case, it may be asked, was there, could there, be any tragedy? Tragedy there was, and very real tragedy; for the irony that mocked His Highness in his latter years was that once it had been gained, he could not recognise the devotion he had earned in full measure from his subjects. When at first he had trusted, they had doubted. When at last they trusted, he not merely doubted, he suspected.

But at the moment none anticipated tragedy. People were far more interested in the question as to the selection His Highness would make for his Chief Minister. Would it be a Dinkar Rao or another Khadke? It proved to be neither. Conjecture in Lashkar was soon set at rest. There was to be no *Diwan!*

Instead a Secretariat was formed with Sir Michael Filose at its head, but though he, as Chief Secretary, had certain powers, comparatively limited powers be it said, every important case went up with the Secretariat notes to His Highness for his personal orders. Sir Michael was no longer a young man and, according to a view often expressed by His Highness, seldom made any note on a file except "I agree with the opinion of the Under-Secretary." That his Under-Secretaries were far from inspired and that the Chief Secretary had no individuality was the comment often made by his colleagues.

The Maharaja, however, viewed this peculiarity from another angle. To Sir Michael he attributed a benign Machiavellism. In owning a sense of obligation to the veteran, he thus expatiated on his intense and true loyalty:—"I can never repay Sir Michael for his profound fidelity. He never did any work himself in order that I should learn to shoulder responsibility, that I should do all for myself and thus gain insight, knowledge, and experience, and acquire self-reliance." This remark was in no ways intended to be sarcastic; it naively voiced a conviction that His Highness nursed deep in his heart.

The next amazing innovation was that the Ruler studied his files by himself! He did not ask some confidential officer or clerk what was the matter needing settlement, still less what was the proper order to be written out for his signature. Sitting alone in his office, he went through each case, made his decision and wrote it out in his large and rather untidy handwriting.

The Secretariat soon found that it was dangerous for their notes on any case to omit a relevant point. Such an omission was brought to their attention sharply, even though, whatever the failing committed, their master at this period and for many years to come was to display a most long suffering disposition.

The institution of the Secretariat under the control of which one civil department after another was brought in rapid succession, resulted almost immediately in a tightening up of the administration as well as in a closer co-ordination of policy.

One of the earliest acts of the Maharaja on attaining his powers was to abolish the pernicious system of "news-writers." These were ill-paid irresponsible persons, one or more in each sub-district of the State, who for a pittance sent in reports about the administration of their particular *Pargana*. In other words, they were individuals independent of the district authorities, paid spies whose business was to bear true or false tales against all Darbar officials away from the capital. It is needless to say that this ancient system had time and again lent itself to blackmail. Madhav Rao Scindia wished to show that until he personally found one of his officers guilty of some malpractice, he was prepared to trust the man on the spot.

This innovation did not mean that the *Subas*, *Tehsildars*, and other district officials were left without a check. Inspired possibly by the excellent work of Sir Michael Filose in Malwa, His Highness created for North and for Central Gwalior two more posts of *Sar-Subas* whose duties were mainly the inspection of the work done by officers in the revenue, judicial, and police departments within their *Prant* or division.

But far more effective even than these new officers were the personal tours of Scindia himself. No Indian Prince of recent years had or ever has been so energetic a traveller in his own dominions. These journeys on horseback from one end of the State to the other were no royal progresses nor mere shooting expeditions. The retinue was kept down to the smallest limits consistent with efficiency, indeed few persons could have kept up with the restless energy of His Highness.

He was everywhere, riding long distances each day, inspecting the work of revenue officers in the fields, seeing what ruined tanks were worthy of repair, suggesting new ones (he had a natural eye for the site of a dam) chatting to or arguing with all sorts and conditions of persons, *zamindar*, *bania*, or *ryot*, watching, perhaps helping, the police to round up dacoits, looking into the distress caused by the failure of the rains in the Isagarh Division and starting relief works, chiefly new roads and *bunds*, showing impatience that the Ujjain-Bhopal line was not yet opened, as the Bina-Goona section had just been, sanctioning extensions to the both those projects, seeing what new buildings were required and where better communications were urgently needed, and in every way by his genuine enthusiasm stirring even the most phlegmatic of his officers into at least a semblance of real activity.

A very typical note issued after the return from one of these earlier tours detailed the fact that *Subas* and *Tehsildars* were too prone to stick to their headquarters and did not move about on inspections of their districts. These officers were enjoined to keep diaries showing where they went and what they did on each working day and submit each diary every month to the Secretariat. At this time there were nineteen *Subats* and sixty-eight *Tehsils*, but in the beginning at least the Maharaja went through each diary personally!

The first tours revealed that many circulars issued by the Council of Regency were not understood and still more were not being followed, that great laxity had been shown during past years in allowing the usurpation of State lands by fictitious *muafi* grants, a matter into which Colonel Pitcher was instructed to look, and that there was a need for the preparation of Civil, Criminal, and Revenue Codes.

This work of codification was taken in hand and very rapidly pushed through, as too was the preparation of a Police Act and Manual.

Long suffering as His Highness then was, his inspection tours had shown him that many of his officers were in no way fitted for the modern administration which was being forced on them. To repair this defect he caused the opening of a Service School to prepare students and especially Maratha boys for future posts in the revenue, police, and judicial departments. This was the first of several special schools started by the late Maharaja. A utilitarian rather than an educative institution, it was organised on lines which showed all the strength and all the weakness of its founder's views on education generally. As he often said, he judged by results; he wanted something practical and he wanted that something in a hurry. He never allowed any boy in whom he was interested to follow his natural bent; the lad must go into whatever department, civil or military, it was his choice to select for him. But a more serious miscalculation, due possibly to his own native versatility, was his persistent failure to recognise the necessity of a sound basis of general education as a preliminary to successful specialisation.

Admittedly the Marathas, his own caste fellows, were backward in education, but it is doubtful if their most deserving cause was really helped by giving them a cramming in the letter of administrative rules and regulations, the spirit of which they could not well appreciate owing to their lack of general grounding.

During its career of many years, while the Service School turned out a number of capable officers, it turned out alas! a far greater number of persons who failed to come up to the administrative ideals of its founder. To its credit, however, may be put the fact that once and for all it shattered the general idea, still current in Gwalior in the early 'nineties that appointment to one of the upper grades of the State Civil Service rested rather on a letter of recommendation and the servile flattery of superiors than on any special merit in the candidate for appointment.

The spring of 1895 saw the first employment of the Imperial Service Troops on active service. On the 25th of March a wire from the Viceroy asked if the Gwalior Transport Corps could join the Chitral Relief Expedition. By the morning of the 29th the last of the Corps had been despatched from Lashkar. The Corps did not return until the autumn and during its absence rendered very creditable service.

During the first two years after the conferment of his powers, Madhav Rao Scindia was particularly fortunate in the retention at the Residency of Colonel Donald Robertson for the greater part of this period. Chief and Political Officer toured together in the State and His late Highness never concealed his gratitude for the excellent lessons in administration which he learned from the colonel's experience and tact.

Major MacIvor, who followed at the Gwalior Residency, in turn won the appreciation of the young Maharaja, but after the untimely death by cholera of this officer the relations between the Residency and the Darbar grew more formal.

It is impossible to avoid a reference to the fact that the immediate successors of Colonel Robertson and Major MacIvor's failed consistently to establish and maintain the close personal touch with His Highness that had been customary during the four or five preceding years. It would be ungracious and it is unnecessary to attempt to apportion the blame for this unfortunate development. Those were not the days in which the Government of India made any definite effort to discover whether the Resident whom they proposed to appoint to a State was the person whom the Chief was anxious to have as his Political Officer. Probably in any case at this time the Maharaja would have been considered too much of a boy to have had any real views as to which particular individual was the most suitable to represent the Supreme Government at the Residency in Morar.

Perhaps the Prince was on occasions inclined to be touchy, maybe the Political Officers of the time too prone to stand on their dignity and, from the vantage ground of middle age, unable to make sufficient allowances for impetuous youth. Happily the Agent to the Governor-General in Central India at this time was His Highness' old friend, Sir David Barr. In Indore at least the Maharaja was sure of sympathetic consideration while in Gwalior he could rely on the loyal and affectionate assistance of the three lent officers, Colonels Crofts and Pitcher and Mr. Johnstone.

It was fortunate that he had such friends and helpers, for already he was attempting to do too much work himself. Details needed attention. To introduce a modern administration into Gwalior within a decade was no easy task. Though their Ruler's efforts were in all cases designed for their own good, his subjects had not yet developed any measure of public opinion which might make the labour easier, while hitherto the powers invested in the Chief Secretary and the district officers were so small that an unnecessarily large number of files were perforce submitted to the Maharaja for his personal orders.

The creation of a Revenue Board had, it is true, proved some relief; for it would have been beyond the mortal power of any single man to clear off the accumulated arrears in the Land Revenue Department alone. In spite of the work done, or supposed to have been done, by the Council of Regency, there were, when the Revenue Board came into existence, more than four hundred cases which had been pending for over ten years, lying untouched since the days of Maharaja Jayaji Rao!

The magnitude of the task of bringing the general administration into line with modern requirements would have been enough to daunt anyone less energetic than Madhav Rao Scindia.

In each department which he scrutinised in person, whether at headquarters or in the districts, he found ignorance, laziness, grave irregularities, and in most instances dishonesty. The organization of the State was still far from complete and many branches of activity were neglected or non-existent. Among these was the administration of the so-called forests. Gwalior had been practically denuded of all fair-sized timber. The woodlands had never been demarcated, and in vast areas of scrub jungle or fodder reserves the villagers cut or burned wood or grass as they pleased.

But the factor which above all else contributed to delay progress was the recurrence of famine. In the year 1895-96 the rains failed in Northern and Central Gwalior. Even Malwa did not have quite its usual bounteous crops. All Rajputana was affected, and through the Gwalior State poured thousand of starving peasants from Jaipur, Udaipur, and Jodhpur, trusting to keep themselves and at least some of their cattle alive until the rains should again fall in the arid and inhospitable wastes they called their homes.

There had been famines in Northern Gwalior before, many of them; but, at all events since the empire of the Moghuls had ceased to be a reality, in the territories now ruled by Scindia, no serious attempt had ever been made by the State to relieve distress. Such of the poverty-stricken folk as were strong enough had been wont to migrate southwards, many never to return alive; the rest too feeble to move had waited at home to die from starvation or from its twin satellites, cholera, and pneumonia.

Anyhow Malwa was safe. There had never been a famine in that province within the memory of man. The very suggestion was unthinkable.

But the young Maharaja was not content to leave the people of the Gwalior and Isagarh Divisions to live or die by their own unaided exertions. Cattle might have to seek food by wandering southwards, but the wholesale migration of men, women, and children with all its resulting panic and its disastrous results must be stopped at any cost.

For the first time in its history the State organised regular relief works for the able-bodied and poor houses for those too feeble or too young to toil. People could hardly understand such an innovation. It might be a deep-laid scheme to persuade them to stay at home and eventually die. The State might think itself over-populated!

Though this first attempt at relief was crude in design and execution, falling far short of the elaborate organisation prescribed in after years by the State Famine Code, the lines on which the task was attempted were in the main very sound. So far as possible all who were fit for labour were given employment within reach of their homes, the works comprising road-construction, the building or repair of irrigation tanks and wells, and, above all, the making of cuttings and embankments for two sections of the Gwalior Light Railways from Lashkar to Sipri and from Lashkar to Bhind.

Money was advanced to the district authorities with orders to see that the starving at least got sufficient food to keep body and soul together, and grants enabling them to purchase seed for the next crop, since necessity had caused the consumption of the usual stocks kept for sowing.

In this manner Scindia developed a policy which has since been accepted in British India; the essential feature being the prevention of migration, so as to ensure a reasonable extent of cultivation when famine came to an end.

The Maharaja was ubiquitous. He moved incessantly inspecting relief works and poor houses, finding fault with the *Subas* or *Tehsildars* who seemed afraid to make use of the funds thus unexpectedly placed at their disposal, seeing that the sums set aside for the necessities of the hungry were neither wasted nor embezzled, and by his own energy generally infusing life into his officers and his subjects.

For once at least in their lives the Gwalior *ryots* got a glimmering of a new conception. For the first time in their experience they had a Ruler who was really concerned whether they lived or died.

The distress in the State was considerably aggravated by an economic change which had taken place in British India. There the mints had been closed and the *Kaldar* or Imperial coin was in consequence rising in value. The chief local coinage in Gwalior, the *Chandori* rupee which had for years been at a discount of nearly three or four per cent, was rapidly depreciating. The time was quietly approaching when it would take nearly one hundred and fifty *Chandori* rupees to buy one hundred of the Imperial currency, and as supplies of grain had to be imported in bulk from British India the cost of such importations in terms of the local money became excessive.

Gradually however the multitudinous difficulties of this famine were surmounted. The rain at last fell in July 1897 and, with the liberal advances made by the State to its cultivators for seed and bullocks, agricultural life in North and Central Gwalior began to recover from the shock.

To-day when the State possesses agricultural banks and a rapidly developing system of co-operative credit societies, the grant of *taccavi* loans to the peasantry seems a very ordinary affair, but it must be remembered that hitherto the State had never come to the rescue of its *ryots*, whose necessities had always forced them to apply to the village money-lender for any such assistance. In the matter of compassion the village *bania* could have learned much even from the gombeenman of Ireland.

The next surprise that came to the agriculturists was the remission of seventy-four lakhs of land revenue, roughly three quarters of the total annual yield of the entire State from this source. Hitherto, whether the *ryot* had reaped a crop or not, the revenue had to be paid and any uncollected arrears would pass on as a burden from year to year, nay from one generation to another, just as did the debt to the money-lender. It is true that the collection of these arrears in full had never proved feasible, but, whenever the peasant had reaped a good harvest, he had been forced to liquidate at least a portion of his outstandings to the State and so could never hope to be free from a crushing load of debt.

In his own interests the money-lender had to some extent helped the Gwalior cultivator through times of scarcity, doubtless on the principle that a live debtor was better than a dead one, but in 1896-97 the famine had been so wide-spread that the *banias* could hardly cope with it; especially as the Chandori rupee by its rapid depreciation had caused a local financial panic in the markets of the State.

The important result achieved was that with the remission of so large a portion of the land revenue the Gwalior *ryot* had begun to pluck up courage. Their Ruler had shown his interest in his people's welfare and the peasants for the first time realised that there was something to be prized in being the subjects of "Madhav Maharaj."

The following agricultural year, 1897-98, was none too prosperous, but at least the cultivators had learned that their lives were of value. In that and the preceding twelvemonth over thirteen million persons, counted by daily units, had been relieved, and thanks to new irrigation tanks and to improved communications generally, a similar failure of the rains could never in future cause the same measure of distress.

In 1897 the Gwalior Transport Corps had again been on active service. The force took a part in the Tirah expedition, and the Maharaja accompanied his troops as far as their base at Khusalgarh where he had had an opportunity of showing that in the case of an accident he was to be depended upon for efficient, if not highly technical, first aid.

The following spring he was summoned to Calcutta for his investiture with the Grand Cross of the Star of India. After that ceremony he returned in haste to the Karera district in the Central Division of his State, there to organise special measures against dacoity which after the famine had assumed undue proportions. Some twenty-five years later he was destined to visit the same district with the same object. That his second advent proved not merely so dramatic but also so effective was due, as will later be told, to the fact that in the intervening time his people had learned to trust him whole-heartedly.

During the year 1898 the State made a good recovery from its famine wounds and stated to carry through an alteration in its currency. While still reserving the right to mint its own coinage, Gwalior adopted as its medium of exchange and measure of value the Imperial or *Kaldar* (milled) rupee. This innovation certainly made commerce with the outer world an easier matter for the State.

The year records progress in other directions. A first attempt at local self-government was made by putting the Lashkar Municipality under the control of a committee instead of keeping it in tutelage as a State department. Though this committee of which His Highness became the president was nominated and not elected, it was entrusted with considerable powers, far greater indeed than the members of the committee appeared anxious to exercise. The president continually had to drive rather than lead his coadjutors in his efforts to instil into them a fraction of his own energy.

Being still dissatisfied with the condition of the Postal Department in his State, the Maharaja at this time himself took a short course in post-office procedure in British India, thus fitting himself to criticise with some knowledge the work of yet another department. This is the last year in which the State Postmaster-General, Pandit Sheo Charan, was able to assert in his administration report that all was for the best in the best of all possible postal departments.

Medical relief in the State was making great strides and education too showing some advance. The first school for girls was opened at Ujjain and was followed shortly by the foundation of the Maharanis' Girls' School in Lashkar. The Sardars' School, an institution for the general education of the sons of the Gwalior nobility, also dates from this year.

As usual, His Highness took little or no relaxation from his duties as a Ruler. In the cold weather of 1898-99, he departed on a long and strenuous tour throughout Malwa: any spare moments were occupied with his office files, the perusal of which convinced him of the dilatory procedure too commonly adopted in the despatch of State work and led to the issue of a Guide Book. The machine was being speeded up; future alterations in its structure would hasten the process.

The year 1899-1900, or Samvat 1956 according to the State calendar, or "*Chhappan-ka-Sal*" to give it its local, ill-omened name, was again a year of calamity. A famine in Malwa was, as all men knew, an impossibility, and yet there actually was a most disastrous famine in this province during these twelve months. The rainfall instead of reaching its normal of over thirty inches varied from a maximum of nine down to less than five in different districts. No Malwa peasant had ever seen a famine at his doors. The province was backward in communications, the people quite unused to irrigation, the population temporarily doubled by the influx of starving wanderers from Rajputana who, as ever, had made for the promised land of plenty, the district officers generally less active than those nearer the capital, and the peasantry, as a whole, physically less robust than the *ryots* of Northern Gwalior.

The outlook was black and the gravity of the position hardly realised in time, for all hope of rain had not been abandoned until the last moment.

Relief works and poor houses were started, but the flood of alien immigration from Rajputana increased in volume. His Highness himself took on the duties of Central Famine Officer.

Even if there had been some delay and unpreparedness at the start, things would now move at last. But the Maharaja fell ill almost immediately and was laid up for a considerable time. He had to give up his post as head of famine relief, but a far more serious disaster was the loss of that energy and drive which were so sorely needed to inspire his servants. Colonel Pitcher, now an elderly man, took over charge and did well, but famine and its handmaid, disease, had got a strong hold: and without His Highness to direct matters the Malwa famine proved more disastrous than that in Northern Gwalior four years earlier. For years afterwards in every Malwa village could be seen houses empty since the dread months of the *Chhappan-ka-Sal*;

to this day in that province are to be found a number of women of no definite caste but clad in men's garb since the famine days when their mothers dressed them as boys in the hope that under the supposition of their being males a greater attempt would be made to save their lives than if they had been mere girls!

Though confined to bed for some months, the Maharaja had not ceased to plan schemes for further development. With the opening by Lord Curzon of the fine Victoria College building in November, 1899, education at the capital had received much encouragement. In the course of this year two new special schools were opened in Lashkar, a Military School for training army officers and a Clerical School to prepare candidates for posts in the State offices.

The South African War had started and an offer from His Highness of trained artillery teams as a free gift had been gratefully accepted by the Government of India.

During his illness the Maharaja had been worrying over administrative problems. Even if things were not so bad as in the past, it was a matter of common knowledge that bribery, peculation, and embezzlement were distressingly common in all branches of the State service. Forbearing as he still was, the Ruler of Gwalior knew that he must take some drastic measures.

Shortly after his recovery, he called a meeting of the most prominent of his Sardars and officers in the Darbar Hall at the Jai Bilas Palace. The proofs of embezzlement in certain cases were incontrovertible. Any law court would have given a conviction, but the effect of a lengthy trial would not, to his thinking, have been so impressive as summary action. Facing Pandit Sheo Charan, the Postmaster-General, and certain subordinate officers of the Palace Department with the proofs of their dishonesty, he extracted confessions of their guilt, and had them led away from the Darbar Hall to the Central Jail to serve lengthy terms of imprisonment.

Whatever may be said of the procedure, there is no doubt that the immediate, indeed the lasting, result of this action was a rapid rise in the general standard of official integrity throughout the State. Honesty began to be regarded as the safest policy.

The next year saw the visit to Lashkar of His Highness the Gaekwar of Baroda. It saw too the first occasion on which any of the Scindia family had left the shores of India for abroad. The Boxer Rising had broken out in China. The State had provided the hospital-ship "Gwalior" for bringing wounded and sick soldiers back from the Far East. His Highness with certain officers of his army went on active service in China, an experience which gave him the keenest pleasure. He returned in excellent health, ready not to enjoy a holiday, but to take up his work in the State just where he had left it off.

If anything, his energy seemed greater than ever. Though he had handed over all judicial appeals to a committee of three senior officials, his total work had increased rather than diminished. His tours in the State were just as arduous and meticulous as they had ever been. He was looking into certain irrigation projects which had failed and by his common-sense now and again pointing out the causes of failure. He was paying particular attention to the training of his troops having doubtless been impressed by his experiences on active service. He was continually forming quick, yet correct and weighty, decisions on a variety of matters, was interesting himself in the investment of certain State balances in British India, paying keen attention to the conclusions to be drawn from the Census of 1901 which showed how Malwa had suffered in the recent famine, and generally doing the work of six men and expecting each of those in his immediate neighbourhood to do the work of three.

This twelvemonth (1901-02) witnessed a visit to Gwalior from the Maharaja of Bikaner and also one from the Commander-in-Chief; it is memorable too for the appointment of His Highness as an A. D. C. to the King-Emperor, an honour he valued more than any other.

Steady progress generally was made by the State, and when in the following year, His Highness paid a short visit to England to attend the Coronation of His Majesty King Edward VII, he was at least satisfied that all was going on well in Gwalior.

He returned an LL. D. of Cambridge University but far more impressed by the motor cars he had seen in Europe than by this academic honour. The first car that he owned is to-day to be seen at the State Museum, a single cylindered 6 H. P. De Dion, which is still in running order, or at least was so when in 1922 it was allowed to retire from regular work.

Though a good sailor (he had already proved himself to be that on his voyage to China), he had found the inaction and lack of exercise on board ship a distinct trial. The organisation of continual deck sports and gymkhanas had been no sufficient outlet for his restless energy. In a happy mood he settled down to work once more. His cold weather tour was as energetic as usual.

The year 1903 brought to him the decoration of the G. C. V. O. It saw too the retirement in the spring of Colonel Pitcher, now an old man. His ability and enthusiasm had served the State excellently for many years, and to this day many of the best features in the revenue administration of Gwalior may be traced to the tactful innovations which he had been instrumental in introducing.

Some two months later Colonel Crofts went on furlough. His previous furlough had been interrupted by his sudden recall to fit out the hospital-ship "Gwalior." The hurried visit to London in 1902 when he had accompanied His Highness had been no real holiday. He certainly deserved this long leave which he was now taking, but there was general lamentation in Gwalior at his departure, for it was common knowledge that the gigantic Irishman would never return to administer the Medical Department and assist the Maharaja in a variety of ways—ways perhaps too varied to be encompassed in the legitimate sphere of his duties as Chief Medical Officer.

CHAPTER VI.

1903–1912

FOR nearly seventeen years Colonel Crofts (to give him his rank at the time) had been in Gwalior performing the joint official duties of Residency Surgeon and Medical Adviser to His Highness. The huge, kind-hearted, if brusque-tempered, Irishman was not merely a very capable physician; he was the Maharaja's counsellor in numerous administrative matters, as well as the director of many of his outdoor hobbies. Ungrudgingly he kept an eye on several State departments where his advice, dictated by blunt common-sense, made for efficiency. For example, to his unofficial interest (such as was only to be expected from one who had so strong a passion for horse-flesh) was due much of the admirable organization of the Animal Department at this time.

The affection between the doctor and the lad who had now grown to manhood was very real, and lasted unbroken until the elder's death in 1915. No European at least ever had a tithe of the influence which the Colonel exercised on Madhav Rao Scindia, an influence too great by far according to the views of the Resident at Gwalior at the time.

So long as Sir David Barr was at Indore any attempts to bring about the removal of Colonel Crofts from Gwalior had failed. That astute Political Officer had been at the Gwalior Residency himself and knew the doctor's worth, indeed had recognised him to be a pivot on which much of the future hopes of the State turned. But on Sir David Barr's promotion to the Hyderabad Residency, a renewed effort by the Political Agent then at Gwalior met with success, and the colonel was transferred in spite of a private appeal from His Highness to Lord Curzon, the Viceroy of the time.

These pages are no place for an assessment of the rights or wrongs of the matter, and, in any case, such an estimate would postulate recourse to papers which are not available for general publication, but even if political expediency justified the transfer, at all events from the point of view of the Maharaja's own health, the action was disastrous.

When ill, His Highness had never submitted to regular treatment from anyone except the colonel, his "*Guruji*" as he had been wont to call him. From the day of Colonel Crofts's transfer, during any periods of ill-health or actual malady, the Maharaja suffered no other doctors to make a fair trial of their science, indeed he always displayed impatience with their methods, however efficacious.

With the departure of the colonel the Gwalior Medical Department was given its separate head, an Indian doctor. This was a deliberate decision of the Maharàja's, not by any means his first step towards replacing European by qualified Indian officers, but by all means a measure conceived to pay off in some degree the unimaginative and thin-skinned Political Officer, as he regarded him, who from a sense of false prestige had engineered the removal of Colonel Crofts from Gwalior.

His Highness strove hard to secure the return of his "*Guruji.*" His prayers fell on sympathetic ears, and the highest in the land made an honest effort to render him satisfaction; but even he was defeated by the serried ranks of prestige and expediency—by the ogre of so-called policy.

This to Madhav Rao Scindia was his first deep disappointment, and filled with the tenacious self-assurance he displayed whenever he conceived himself to be in the right, a peculiarity which was his throughout life, it shook his faith in the sympathy and wisdom of the British Government, if not indeed in their strict impartiality when the choice lay between service traditions and humane common-sense. He vowed that never again should there be a European Chief Medical Officer in Gwalior and clung to his resolution with his characteristic pertinacity. Never again were the posts of Residency Surgeon and head of the State Medical Department united in a single individual. From the day on which Colonel Crofts departed the Maharaja had perforce to rely on himself more than hitherto.

He quickly disproved the idea that his ubiquitous energy had been partly due to the driving power of his "*Guruji.*" He showed, to quote the words of the then Viceroy, that he considered his *Gadi* "not a diwan of indulgence but the stern seat of duty." Apart from his normal tale of daily work, he, at the end of 1903, might have been seen engaged in a minute scrutiny of the drafts of his projected Correspondence and Accounts Manuals, as well as of a Revenue Board Manual, all labours which his keen insight into departmental routine enabled him to undertake with exceptional efficiency.

At this time also he was much occupied with the reorganization of the territorial divisions of the State. Experience had proved the number of *Subats* and *Tehsils* to be excessive, since the introduction of a liberal settlement had made the collection of land revenue a far simpler task than of old. Towards the end of the year he again left his headquarters, and went off on one of his usual strenuous cold weather tours.

During the next year appeared a new crop of manuals or codes, amongst others the *Kanoon Mal,* the Zamindari Manual, the *Kham Dehat* Manual, and the Engineering Code; all of them necessary sets of regulations for an up-to-date administration, yet hardly meriting mention here but for the fact that their most practical provisions originated mainly in the Maharaja's own suggestions or revision.

From this year too dates the creation on modern scientific lines of a State Forest Department as well as the reorganization of the engineering services. Irrigation was progressing too slowly to suit His Highness's ideas. For this branch of civil engineering he insisted on a separate department. Mere submerging tanks were not enough; large storage lakes for perennial canal irrigation were becoming a necessity.

In the history of Scindia's Army the year is memorable for a large increase in the number of Imperial Service Troops supplied by the State. The existing two cavalry regiments were augmented by a third, two battalions of infantry were added, and the transport corps was expanded by the addition of a further hundred carts. By these measures the numbers of the Gwalior Imperial Service Forces were more than doubled.

The agricultural year started well but ended badly. Severe frosts wrought havoc among the *rabi* crops and led to a remission of thirteen lakhs of land revenue.

Now that literacy was making rapid strides in the State, it was in His Highness's view essential that the people of Gwalior should be given an opportunity of learning not only what was happening in the world outside, but also what was being done for them in the State and what was expected of them as loyal subjects. January 1905 saw the birth of the "Jayaji Pratap," a local weekly, which to-day is still in a most flourishing condition. Published partly in the Hindi and partly in English, in later years it developed into an organ which the Maharaja often used for publishing anonymous contributions setting out his personal views on a variety of matters of general or special interest. He was nothing if not versatile, nothing if not an amazingly resourceful propagandist.

A further issue of manuals, each as usual checked in detail by the Maharaja himself, laid down the procedure to be followed in the Forest, Court of Wards, Police, and Jail Departments. Whatever might be the individual capacity of his officers, he determined that the need of continuity of policy should be brought home to all and by authoritative instructions he prescribed a deficiency standard of efficiency, demanding thereby far more than had been expected in the past.

The Christmas of 1905 saw the State honoured by a formal visit from the Prince of Wales and his Consort. Into all the multifarious details demanding arrangement on such an occasion His Highness threw himself with his usual energy; the smallest matter was not too insignificant to receive his personal attention. For the pomp of the State Entry into Gwalior of his Royal guests and the splendour of the formal Darbar, for their personal comfort during their hours of freedom from official ceremony or for the excellence of the *shikar*, the credit was due from the first to the Maharaja's own careful consideration not only of what would happen but of what might happen.

His Royal Highness at the State banquet announced the appointment of the Maharaja as Honorary Colonel of the First Duke of York's Own Lancers (Skinner's Horse). The Maharaja in his speech had fully expressed his appreciation of the honour paid the State by the Royal Visit, and his words rang as true as those of his father in 1876. His chagrin at being given no seat at the banquet owing to the procedure adopted at the time was admirably concealed at the moment, though years later it found an indirect expression in Volume II of the "Policy."

Happily fate had arranged that Gwalior was to have the good fortune of a second visit from His Royal Highness. In the following February the contemplated shoot in the Nepal Terai had to be abandoned at the last moment, and the Prince of Wales came to Gwalior unofficially, and stayed for over two weeks at Sipri.

Those were wonderful days of great sport and unaffected enjoyment for both the heir to the British

Crown and his host. The spontaneous affability which made it natural for His Royal Highness to enter into the local atmosphere and its simple pleasures without the least aloofness, yet without undue familiarity, made the deepest impression on the Maharaja as on all those who were privileged to be in Sipri at the time. If possible, it intensified the passionate devotion of His Highness' to the Royal Family of England. There is little doubt that this memorable fortnight was the happiest in all the Maharaja's life. In his later years, unconsciously imitating his father, he would often recall the joy of that memorable occasion.

Yet apart from social functions the cold weather was a strenuous time for the State generally, since Northern Gwalior was once more in the grip of a severe famine which had been aggravated considerably by the failure of the spring crops in the previous year.

Testimony that the famine administration of the State was now fully adequate to combat the calamity has been received from many sources; but no testimony was so valued as that of His Royal Highness the Prince of Wales who personally visited and inspected the famine camp at Singhanwas near Sipri.

In the form of relief works the extension of the Gwalior Light Railway to Sheopur was pushed on, more roads and irrigation projects were taken in hand, while no less than thirty-two lakhs of land revenue were remitted, so that by these and other means the famine was first scotched and then killed.

Meanwhile, without undue parade, the judiciary and the general administration of law were being raised to a state of efficiency of which Gwalior hitherto had hardly dreamed. By the exertions of a newly appointed Chief Justice in whom His Highness placed complete confidence, the rule of law was becoming a reality in every district of the State. No longer was any interference with the normal course of justice a possibility; there could now be no suggestion that some magistrate was too courtly or that his decisions reflected his own particular view of what would please the Darbar rather than the strictly legal aspect of the case before him. No longer too were revenue officers suffered to exercise any judicial powers in their districts.

Madhav Rao Scindia had given his people security of life and property against dacoity. He had shown that their material comfort and prosperity were his anxious care. They were now for the first time in their lives to receive the boon of speedy justice. Already they had begun to realise that they had a recognisable status, not as inhabitants of a territory called Gwalior, but as the subjects of "Madhav Maharaj."

The famine passed, but the next season was far from favourable to the cultivators. The newly formed Forest Department too had not come up to expectations, and complaints, well or ill founded, were common, necessitating the personal investigation of the Maharaja. Further, the system of State custom duties needed revision, if any commercial progress was to be made. The transit of goods from one part of the State to another was hampered by the existence of over a thousand internal custom posts, service at which did not rank as State Service and was admittedly very corrupt. Better officials were needed for this department, and to meet the want yet another utilitarian school, the Customs Class, was formed, while the alteration of the existing system was being pushed on.

Certain schemes too which had been started shortly before were not doing very well. For example, a reference to the Administration Report for the year 1907-08 shows that the steam ploughs, then being utilised for breaking up old fallow for new settlers, were not working so quickly as had been anticipated.

This report is interesting in many ways. For the first time the introductory remarks of His Highness are of considerable length and in several cases express his dissatisfaction with the progress made by various departments. Though as a whole the work of his officers is praised, yet a reference to this report as compared with its predecessors would seem to show that, while still optimistic, and occasionally unduly so, His Highness was not so happy in his task as he had been. He had been interesting himself in the development of industries in the State, and had conceived the notion, which he never abandoned for all its impossibility, of communication by river with Calcutta; but despite his new projects, he appears dissatisfied with much that had so far been achieved. Things were not moving so rapidly as he had hoped or expected.

A narrow escape from death in a railway accident to his special train in this year he had treated with absolute unconcern, just as he had, as a matter of course, devoted himself to cheering up in the midst of the wreckage the nerve-shattered driver who had been responsible for the accident. The Maharaja still had nerves of iron, his physical health was outwardly as good as ever, but he was beginning to nurse the belief that in his work for the State he was as a rule ploughing a lonely furrow. Perhaps he missed the breezy companionship of Colonel Crofts.

In any case the absence of his "*Guruji*" was a misfortune, for in this year it was definitely decided by the doctors that His Highness was suffering from diabetes. A course of regular treatment was clearly necessary to check the progress of the disease but, now that the colonel was away, the Maharaja was not ready to follow any course of regular treatment. In public affairs he might show the most reasonable of attitudes, but so far as his private life was concerned, he was the complete autocrat.

Nevertheless, well or ill, he did not slacken his work. New projects were continually being revolved in his mind. An up-to-date State must to his thinking be industrial, so the year 1908-09 saw a great effort at commercial development. The young Commerce and Industry Department set about establishing various new factories with the idea that such concerns, once they had proved financial successes, might be handed over to companies or private individuals for management.

Though reference will again on several occasions be made to subject, it may be stated here that unquestionably it was in the line of commercial development that Madhav Rao Scindia's greatest failures are to be found. To his death he would never believe that State agency is unsuited to the creation of any industry, nor that official routine is the step-mother of business, and this in spite of the fact in his everyday files he was always pointing out the lethargy induced by what he called the "red-tape-worm." While shrewd in business matters generally, he was ever too prone to listen to the wiles of unscrupulous persons or to the optimism of incompetents who promised with the surplus balances of the State to turn Lashkar into a Manchester or (a reference to the Chambal Navigation Scheme) into a London.

While his increasing office work tied him more and more to his capital, His Highness in industrial matters was inclined to neglect the obvious possibilities of Ujjain, the one town in his State above all others which presented real scope for commercial advancement.

With a reorganised system of customs administration, Gwalior might have achieved considerable progress in trade, but a lack of any acquaintance with economic science disabled His Highness from appreciating the fact that the incidence of export duties is on the producer of the article exported or that the "Mercantile Theory," which heresy he evolved anew for himself, was not the latest creed of modern political economy.

By his unfortunate experiments in State-run or State-aided business ventures he certainly delayed the commercial development of Gwalior in a considerable measure, and the pathos of his failure lies in the fact that each new undertaking was genuinely intended by him to increase the wealth of his subjects.

Even Sipri, a small town some seventy odd miles south-west of the capital, whither for several years he had been wont to go for some slight relief from the summer heats of Lashkar, was, if possible, to grow into a commercial city. This old British cantonment which had been handed back to the State in 1896, saw in the summer of 1909 the first new buildings for what the Maharaja designed should be the headquarters of himself and his chief officers during the hot weather.

The scheme developed rapidly, if at first without any rigid plan, just as yearly additions to the so-called palace at Sipri turned that building from three disconnected bungalows set on a ridge into a queer-shaped mass of masonry, possessed of no architectural plan nor cohesion. Yet it was roomy and suited His Highness admirably.

The climate of Sipri, while certainly cooler than that of Lashkar in hot months, is at its best in the rains; the surrounding country with its wood-clad hills is not merely full of big game but is generally most picturesque. Yet when His Highness first began to develop his idea of a summer capital, it is doubtful if any of his Sardars or officers realised the full possibilities of the place as already visualised by their master.

The growth of Sipri to which allusion will again be made was certainly the work which gave the Maharaja the greatest pleasure in his latter years, and to this day there is not in the whole area a single official residence the site of which was not chosen by His Highness personally. Yet it was always a grief to him that, in the quarter he had set aside for factories, few chimneys rose to belch out smoke to the skies!

Sipri or Shivpuri, to give the town its present name, with its unæsthetic houses for officers, situate for the most part amid rather monotonous surroundings, but possessing in its fine lake a delightful expanse of water enringed by enchanting scenery, may be held to represent the ideas of its modern creator. By his energy this summer capital developed from a spot in which State officials had at first to endure considerable discomfort into a place where the amenities of modern life were at least available; and the original prejudice against the scheme, a prejudice that many held, has to-day passed into a general admission that Sipri is a real asset in the hot weather and rains.

On no ground, however, could Sipri be regarded a suitable site for an industrial centre, and happily there is little fear that its natural beauties will be seriously damaged by unromantic factory buildings, in this or succeeding generations.

From the first the climate of the place appeared to suit His Highness better than that of Lashkar. Had his life been spared, it is more than probable that Sipri eventually would have been proclaimed the official capital. In any case the prosecution of what at first seemed merely the whim of their Ruler has left for his officers and subjects generally a place which, for all its extravagances and its occasionally pathetic attempts at aping the distractions of the big hill station, is a spot of beauty in which to-day real work and genuine enjoyment are not so hard to secure as they seemed at first.

What if, in places, corrugated iron abuts on beautifully carved stone work? Or if, in certain cases, through undue haste money was wasted on such buildings as the military lines? At a period when, owing to ill-health, Madhav Rao Scindia found little joy in life, he at least experienced the bliss of a creator who built a town according to his own taste and was not dissatisfied with the result. There are advantages in being born with utilitarian rather than artistic tastes.

The year 1909-10 witnessed a great advance in irrigation. Having decided on the necessity for large protective works, the Maharaja placed the State Irrigation Department in charge of Mr. Sidney Preston who had just retired from the control of the corresponding department in the Government of India.

During the preceding twelvemonth had been started an ambitious scheme by which the seasonal flow of the Sank and Asan rivers in northern Gwalior was to be impounded by four large dams and the water distributed by canals over a large area. It was by far the biggest project that had as yet been devised for the State and was designed to render a large part of the Bhind District immune from famine. In addition a number of smaller schemes were also in progress and had received considerable impetus from the plentiful supply of casual labour available during the famine of 1905-06 and the scarcity of 1906-07.

From the Administration Report for 1909-10 it can be seen that for once His Highness was satisfied with the speed at which irrigation works were being pushed on, but several other State departments and in particular that of Commerce and Industry were severely criticised. There can be found complaints, which later became so common, that the attention to previous orders paid by certain officers was not all that it should have been, and that new officials on entering the service did not make a point of studying the procedure laid down for particular departments nor of acquainting themselves with the instructions of the Darbar scattered through departmental records.

The official year closed sadly with the news of the death of His Majesty Edward VII. It had seen the Maharaja working as hard as ever, but owing to ill-health, not so equal to the self-imposed strain as in early days. In any case Gwalior was making steady progress and, thanks to the fact that various Political Officers who about this time held charge of Gwalior Residency had been sympathetic enough to recognise the reality of the ungrudging efforts made by His Highness on his people's behalf, the relations between the Darbar and the Residency were again cordial instead of being merely correct.

In the summer of 1911 came the call to London for the Coronation of the King-Emperor George V which it was necessary for His Highness to attend in his capacity of A. D. C. to His Majesty. Before leaving for England the Maharaja handed over the care of the State to his mother, the Dowager Maharani

Sahiba, and scrupulous to observe personally the regulations laid down by him for his own officers, prepared his "Charge Sheet," in reality a memorandum encyclopedic in its size and contents.

This document surveyed the whole field of State administration, took stock of the past progress achieved in each department, indicated the lines of future advance, and specifically noted down matters to be worked up during the bare three months during which he purposed to be out of India. The document wound up with an exhortation to the officers of Gwalior to sink all private or individual differences and to work together harmoniously for the good of the State.

In His Highness' suite was Mr. Johnstone, who was now about to retire after more than twenty years of faithful service in Gwalior. "Masterji" was, on his arrival in England, to be attached as Political Officer to his old pupil during the Maharaja's stay in England. This appointment was much appreciated by His Highness and his suite generally.

It is unnecessary here to recapitulate the various official ceremonies in which His Highness took part as A. D. C. to His Majesty or to give an account of the many social functions he attended. Two Universities, Oxford and Edinburgh, conferred on him the degrees of D. C. L. and LL. D., respectively, honours which interested him chiefly from the ceremonial employed on each occasion. It is doubtful if to the end of his life the Maharaja was ever quite sure which of his academic honours was the gift of which University; but he always remembered that the Latin speech on his presentation at Oxford was longer than that which had been delivered at Cambridge in 1902!

His departure from England was marked by a gift of £ 8,000 to the King-Emperor for distribution among charitable institutions at His Majesty's pleasure. By an exploit at Hurlingham of which mention will be made in another place, His Highness had come prominently before the public eye, indeed he had been distinctly annoyed by the comments of the Press and especially by the title of "Hero of Hurlingham" given him by a sporting journalist with a taste for alliteration.

The visit to Europe had been all too short and too crowded with engagements to be any real holiday. It had been presumed in Gwalior that the three months' absence would probably be extended to six, but the middle of August saw His Highness back in Gwalior and at work immediately.

This speedy return surprised people all the more since it was by this time fairly general knowledge that the Maharaja had left a *fiancée* in England. His Highness had been wedded for over nineteen years, but his marriage had not been blessed by children. In accordance with usual Hindu custom many of his friends had urged him to contract a second alliance. The past history of Gwalior had afforded several instances to prove the truth of the old saying "woe to the land when a child is king." The people of the State did not relish the prospect of the future adoption of some minor who might grow up into a good or bad prince. Yet in spite of various attempts at persuasion, His Highness had hitherto refused to consider the idea of a second marriage.

In England, however, his views would seem to have altered. Circumstances had led to his closer acquaintance with the only daughter of His Highness the Gaekwar of Baroda, and a recent friendship had developed into something deeper. The engagement of one prominent Maratha Prince with the daughter of another had been one of the features of the London season and had given the papers an interesting item for their social columns.

In India in high political circles, the idea of this domestic alliance had been frankly viewed with apprehension, if not with dismay. No suspicion was, of course, voiced, none could be, but those behind the scenes remember the flutter in the dovecots.

The unwavering and fundamental loyalty of the Gaekwar to the British Crown had not yet been fully vindicated, as it has since been in ample measure. He is a taciturn, sensitive, and shy man with the hyperæsthesia of honourable intention. More widely read and travelled than most Ruling Princes, he is withal intellectually curious. In the belief that his motives could never be suspect, he had sought to study the psychologies of Indian Mazzinis, and to understand their ideals and aspirations, had not forborne to make the acquaintance of Syamji Krishna Varmas and Mesdames Camas.

An alliance between the two leading Maratha houses, both among the richest of Indian States, the head of one avowedly identified with the welfare of the British Crown and that of the other with a credited *penchant* for dallying with undesirables, such a union might, it was thought, not turn out for the good of India. Might not the elder Prince with his advanced views influence the younger and wean him from his hereditary allegiance? It was a fascinating subject for discussion among those whose interest in local politics is attracted mainly by the field those politics offer for gloomy forebodings, unworthy suspicions, and counsels of despair.

Scindia knew all this. He had faith in his caste-fellow and peer because he knew him better than the critics. He was fired with the ambition to prove that his relation-to-be was not only untainted but grossly misjudged. Scindia trusted to his own personality to compel the recognition of this fact and thereby to render signal service to the British Government.

The unstaged drama merited open presentation for all the world to see. On the one side was unspoken dread, on the other sanguine confidence to which utterance was not given. Both were in conflict and bursting to find opportunity to prove themselves.

The enterprise miscarried, the test never came, but to the credit of Madhav Rao Scindia be it said that he had judged correctly, as subsequent history has proved. It is to-day difficult to realise how black were the clouds of misapprehension and suspicion lowering at that moment. Dramatically for one short scene they grew even blacker, but then rapidly dispersed and left behind the clear blue sky in which by the grace of Heaven mistrust and wrongful judgment cannot obscure the bright light of truth.

His Highness had been anxious that the wedding should be celebrated while he was still in England, but the elaborate ceremonies attendant on the simplest of Hindu marriages would have presented much difficulty so far as their performance out of India was concerned. Not unreasonably the parents of the bride objected to so unconventional a proceeding. There must be no suspicion of unorthodoxy about the contemplated alliance upon which so much might depend.

So, as usual, putting his public duties before his private predilections, the Maharaja left Europe for Gwalior. As finally arranged, the wedding was to take place at Baroda early in 1912 after the various functions in connection with the forthcoming Delhi Darbar were well over.

To those who were most intimate with him His Highness appeared to have conquered his old objection to a second marriage; he seemed indeed to be anticipating the new alliance with complete happiness, but, for all that, his attention to public affairs showed no lessening of interest. He was at this time much occupied with the question of various "guaranteed estates" the holders of which, thanks to the neglect of Gwalior officers in former times and encroachments on the State's prerogatives, encroachments rendered easy by the willing sympathy of representatives of the Government of India, had of recent years been arrogating to themselves rights which were justified neither by past history nor even by modern political expediency.

On this question the decision of which took over a decade His Highness felt very keenly, for it touched the matter of his prerogative. He considered his legitimate rights were being questioned, if indeed they were not being whittled away, and he had studied the past political history of the State sufficiently to recognise that inattention to the maintenance of the old prerogatives of the house of Scindia had resulted in their diminution, owing to the self-complacent apathy of his predecessors, since the days of his namesake the great Mahadji. "Let the Supreme Government give me my legitimate rights and, in their time of need, all that I have is theirs" was a phrase often on his lips and words expressive of a very genuine sentiment.

Apart from the "guaranteed holders" the case of his other *jagirdars* was engaging much of his attention. These holders of land had very definite rights as vassals of their suzerain, Scindia, but they also had duties. The fact that their ancestors had received grants of territory or cash allowances for services rendered did not to the mind of the Maharaja import that the present-day holders were absolved from all liability to help the State by their service. They were exactly the class which he wanted to associate with himself in the labour of Government. For this reason he had established the Sardars' School, a special institution for their education, and had time and again publicly promised that, should the product of this school prove its fitness, he would advance them to the highest posts in the administration.

It is probably about this time that His Highness first seriously developed the idea that, because Education did not quickly turn out the product he desired, something must be wrong with Education. He recognised that environment did play a big part in life, but refused to the end ever to admit that heredity is the greatest force of all in the making of citizens.

Meanwhile he took a keen interest in the preparation of the "History of the Jagirdars," a comprehensive compilation dealing with each separate estate and its holder, and pointing out in definite terms the rights and duties of each vassal.

The month of December saw His Highness at Delhi for the King-Emperor's Darbar and in attendance on his Sovereign at Calcutta during the Christmas week. Meanwhile most elaborate arrangements were being made to celebrate his approaching marriage, not only in Baroda but in Gwalior as well.

It was less than a month before the actual date fixed for the wedding that it became known that the marriage would not take place. No formal announcement of this fact was ever made. The engagement had been broken off at the request of the Baroda Princess and this was the most that came to the knowledge of the public.

Grimly Madhav Rao Scindia took the blow, at all events with outward calmness. He returned, if with weariness, yet with increased determination, to his office files and his schemes for the betterment of his State.

CHAPTER VII.

1912–1918

THE year 1912 was no happy one for India generally. In Bengal sedition was rife and culminated in an attempt on the life of Lord Hardinge when making his ceremonial entry into Delhi as Viceroy. None the less, Gwalior, where the idea, almost the word, "Sedition," was unknown, made steady progress.

Yet the Ruler of the State was far from happy. The twelvemonth had started badly with the frustration of his hopes in the matter of his marriage with the Baroda Princess. Apart from any sentimental reasons, this undreamt-of eventuality had come as a shattering blow to his self-esteem.

The diabetes in his system was making progress, although its course was from time to time checked by desultory treatment. That no regular methods could be adopted for its cure was not the fault of his medical attendants, but must be put down to the credit of an idiosyncrasy inherited from his father. For a few days he might adhere to the prescription of some physician trained in western lines of medicine. Then he would follow the Ayurvedic system of cure propounded by some Hindu *vaidya*, only on the morrow to abandon it for Unani methods suggested by a Mohammedan *hakim*. At times he might even follow two or three mutually antagonistic lines of treatment at once or oftener still neglect them all. In any case, he took none of them very seriously and refused to submit to a regular diet.

He had been stoutish, but he now became thinner. He still rode nearly every morning, but had given up the games he had been wont to play, and no longer was an enthusiastic competitor in the various events organised by the Gwalior Gymkhana Club or its successor, the Sports Club.

As a matter of fact, he was so busy with office files that he seldom rose from his study table until the day-light was fading, and it was too late for exercise. Then perhaps for relaxation he would motor out to Sakhya Vilas, a pretty little pleasure-house, a mile or so distant from the Jai Bilas Palace. Yet even then, as likely as not, in the car he was driving he had one or two files which he had not so far disposed of, and over these he would ponder or would send a message post-haste to some officer or officers to hurry to Sakhya Vilas, and, on his or their arrival, would sit discussing new schemes or lines of policy until it was long past his usual dinner hour.

Every scheme or policy had as its foundation the idea of the improvement of the State whether in administration or in the material wealth of its people. He never seemed able to get away from the conviction, which usually is but a passing sensation with most people, that there was so much to do and so little time to do it in. It is doubtful if this feeling is really conducive to successful accomplishment. It requires results, speedy results, to satisfy it, and even then it remains insatiable.

In his thirty-page introduction to the volume dealing with the Administration of the Gwalior State for the year 1912-13 there first occurs the expression of his dictum which later grew to be almost his motto that he "judged by results." He reviews the work of every department and finds little that is satisfactory in any one of them. The pathos of the situation was that, while few persons would have claimed that all was well in the State of Gwalior, a vast amount of successful work had been done and was in process of being done, but His Highness was temperamentally unable to contrast the condition of the moment with a less satisfactory past. He must contrast it with an imagined and far more advanced future and made himself unhappy with the thought that the present was nowhere near that visionary standard of perfection.

Perhaps because the advance hitherto made was so much the result of his personal exertions, he would allow little or no credit for the leeway already made up.

In certain respects the introduction to the Administration Report for this year reads as if it might have been written a decade later when mental gloom had wrapped him deeper in its folds.

Undoubtedly there was some cause for discouragement. The Commerce and Industry Department was making no real progress, except in the art of producing a lengthy statement of its activities for the year, but elsewhere a general advance was being made, to judge from a comprehending study of each departmental report.

Yet the Maharaja could not see this. He complains in his review that orders already issued were not being carried out, and that new officers on joining the State service did not sufficiently acquaint themselves with the Darbar's policy, but wished to introduce as innovations methods already prescribed!

He too had been devoting his attention to various political cases recently put up to the Government of India and considered, as was later admitted, that accident and lapse of time, if not policy, had infringed on some of his prerogatives as Ruler of Gwalior. In certain instances he traced this not so much to the carelessness of State officials in the past as to the opportunity given during minorities for the whittling down of ancient, if inconvenient, State rights. The next year was to see his suggestion—it later bore fruit—that the Government of India should make a clear statement as to what their attitude would be in the case of minority administrations in the Native States generally.

The Maharaja had been watching with dismay the momentary outcrop of sedition in the schools and colleges in many parts of British India. There was no sign, there has never been any real sign, of such a tendency in any of the Gwalior educational institutions, but His Highness writes as if he was already face to face with such a calamity. The budget of the Education Department had received some considerable increase in the previous year; but he was definite in his pronouncement that unless the schools produced loyal citizens, they would without hesitation be closed.

The following year saw some slight improvement in the Maharaja's health and a resumption of more optimistic views.

On May 8, 1913, he had contracted a second marriage with a member of the well-known and highly respected Rane family of Goa. He saw the necessity for a son of his own whom he could train, and wanted no adopted child to continue his work in Gwalior. The wedding ceremony was carried out very quietly and caused hardly a break in the daily routine of his work;

but that work was assuming such proportions as to make it practically impossible for any one man to finish it, however able and industrious he might be. His methods and habit made him scrutinise each little detail, and hitherto he had entrusted comparatively small powers to the Secretariat in dealing with any cases which came up from the various subordinate departments.

By administrative changes now introduced he replaced three secretaries by six members with portfolios, and considerable powers were given to the new officers to dispose of unimportant cases. Yet it is doubtful if this innovation, though it certainly made for increased efficiency in the government, really gave the Maharaja much rest. The administrative wheel turned quicker than ever and in practice the members had merely been appointed to speed its revolution. It was true that His Highness was now relieved of much petty routine work, but the files that still came up to him were increasing in complexity, if not in number, and he got no real relief from his burden.

He would never entertain the suggestion of a *diwan*. The very word brought to his mind Ganpat Rao Khadke and nothing else. He needed rest, but a rapid motor tour of inspection over every mile of road in his State was no relaxation. Increased speed in travelling had only enabled him to inspect more of his State within a fixed period. His examination of the work of district offices, schools, or hospitals was as meticulous as ever, but his criticisms had grown more mordant. His malady was gaining ground. Somehow he needed relief from purely State work, and Fate ordained that he should find it for some four years.

In August 1914 the Great War blazed up with dire suddenness. In Gwalior at least its eruption had not been anticipated, even if an increasing number of globe-trotting military officers from Germany had of recent years been evincing an interest in the archæological remains of Gwalior. Some of the more inquisitive of this company had been privileged to watch certain of the irregular forces of the State at their drill and, if they chose to carry away the idea that these picturesque survivals of an earlier day were the flower of Scindia's Army, there was none whose special duty it was to enlighten them as to their error. It is not Indian etiquette to remove officiously the misapprehensions of a visitor, and, in any case, a globe-trotter seldom shows gratitude for any correction suggested to his point of view. If again on being taken to Sussera to shoot a black-buck, some German Staff officer chose to mistake a shikari for an N. C. O. in some Gwalior Regiment, the mistake might be allowed to pass unnoticed. After all the shikari was a man in *khaki*.

During his short period of active service in China, His Highness, rightly or wrongly, had formed no high opinion of the forces of the Fatherland. From a close personal friendship with Lord Kitchener who had paid several visits to Gwalior, the Maharaja was prepared to place complete confidence in the Field-marshal's estimate. Kitchener prophesied that the war would be a long one. If he said so, Madhav Rao Scindia was convinced that statement must be well founded. At no time, even when the cause of the Allies looked to be at its nadir, did the Maharaja fail in his confidence that success would at last attend their arms.

It has been said above that His Highness needed relief from the excess of office work in which of late years most of his waking hours had been spent. During the full four years of the struggle he got some respite, not from activity—that would have killed him—but from too much desk routine. There was in charge of India a Viceroy for whom from their first meeting he had conceived a deep personal affection. To the Residency too was shortly to return a Political Officer whom he was able to regard as a friend and fit in his opinion to be classed with the sympathetic counsellors of his youth.

The prominent part that the Maharaja was able to play in the prosecution of war activities, not merely in his own State, but in India as a whole led continually to his absence from Gwalior for a few days at a time,

He had to make constant railway journeys, and it was a peculiarity of his constitution that travel by train always seemed to suit his health rather than to tire him.

But above all his jaded nerves and constitution were recreated by the idea that the great occasion had come. He would not miss his opportunity. Time and again he had said to prominent personages in the political world "Give me my bare rights, and in your time of danger all that I have is yours," but he was not going to make his rights the condition for his assistance now that the danger had come.

At the banquet, given in Gwalior in 1905 to Their Royal Highnesses who were now seated on the British Throne, he had uttered the words: "It will be enough for me to say that whatever useful work has been or is being done in the various departments of my State it has one ultimate goal, namely, to help towards the stability of the British Empire," and again: "My hope and ambition are that the day may come when my Army and I may by our acts show what is not only on our lips but in our hearts."

Such professions were to Scindia no mere conventional expressions nor facile lip-service. They were spoken with genuine sincerity, with passionate loyalty.

What if his artillery consisted of antiquated muzzle-loading pieces and if his requests for something at least a little more up to date had been refused by the Government of India from considerations of "policy"? At least his gun teams were as well horsed and trained as those of an ordinary British battery. The three hundred artillery horses given in the South African War had proved that this estimate was not far wrong. He could and did give his Waler teams again.

What if he had been told, rightly or wrongly, that a prominent political officer had given to a far more important personage his estimate that Scindia was "the most seditious of all the Indian Princes?" By his acts Scindia could prove such a judgment to be a lie.

He wired to the Viceroy placing the whole resources of his State at the command of the British Government. He offered too his personal services.

In reviewing the events of the next four years it seems providential that his malady rendered void the original proposal that Scindia should proceed on active service, as did some of the Indian Princes. While doubtless he might have performed some nominal military duties in France with success, his personality could never have had full scope in any staff billet, even if his physical ailment had not ensured his speedy return to India as unfit.

But this did not prevent him from dreaming of independent command! A fond hope, but one earnestly entertained. He yearned to prove himself, and his eyes were set on German East Africa. Outside the circle of his intimates few knew that, were his heart's wish granted, his apparent hesitancy to go to the front would have in an instant changed to avidity. He would have gone, probably to bring about a disaster and give his life, possibly, had his luck held, to surprise the world in some original way and win lasting glory.

It seems unfair, however, to lift the veil further and thereby perhaps to court posthumous ridicule for one who had dared to rate himself so highly. In any case his dreams were those of a sick man whose health would have precluded all hope of his bearing the hardships of an active campaign, but it is certain that fear was not the soporific which induced such dreams.

Still in Gwalior, indeed in the wider sphere of India, his prevision and his abilities found a magnificent field for display. In his State the Maharaja had to make rapid and weighty decisions. For a year or two before the outbreak of the War those most nearly connected with him had noticed that on occasions he had begun to evince a difficulty in making up his mind on some official matter, a difficulty which had never been noticeable in the earlier years of his rule.

With the commencement of hostilities any such signs of indecision vanished in a moment. Mentally he was back on the firm pedestal of foresight and determination on which he had been so firmly set a decade before.

These pages are no place in which to record the doings of the Gwalior Imperial Service Troops during the War, though there is ample testimony from qualified military authorities that they played their part manfully in France, East Africa, Egypt, Salonika, Palestine and Mesopotamia, apart from their employment in garrison duties and remount training in British India or in active service on the frontier. It was not possible for His Highness, as he had wished, to see their work and discipline in actual warfare. Suffice it to say that their numbers were kept up to full strength until the Armistice and this in spite of the supply of several thousand recruits to the Indian Army from the Gwalior State.

A lengthy, but incomplete, account of the assistance rendered to the cause of the Allies is published in a book entitled "Gwalior's Part in the War." The extraordinary expenditure incurred by the State on account of the War aggregated nearly twenty-five million rupees. A repetition of the details of the free gifts given or services rendered would fill pages but would merely be wearisome.

The point worthy of recognition is that the originator in every case, whether a gift was offered or any service rendered, was His Highness himself. Not that he ever claimed any personal credit for his performances. In his speeches on several occasions he insisted that it was State money that was being used, and that any merit for its expenditure should be considered as due to his subjects, not to himself.

While there was money in the State Treasury it was easy enough to pour it out. To loan fifty lakhs free of interest to the Indian Government, to postpone an annual payment of thirty-eight lakhs due from that Government to the Darbar, to provide thirty-five lakhs of silver coin in exchange for sovereigns when the Indian exchequer was running low and there was a fear that the paper currency might become inconvertible, to supply an additional half crore of silver specie and a still larger amount in silver bullion, all such assistance His Highness treated as a matter of course.

It was in other arrangements, such as ready co-operation with the Government of India in husbanding the resources of the State with a view to economic control and in the supply of war materials, that the Maharaja's peculiarly intimate knowledge of his own dominions proved of so much value.

His personal gifts and contributions of various kinds for the prosecution of the War came to nearly forty lakhs, and it is over some of these that a short pause may be made, for each was the result of his careful investigation and innate common-sense. For example, there was no waste over war charities that led nowhere, no subscriptions to societies to look after the welfare of those "war babies" whom England in a fit of sentimental wrong-headedness decided must be born in extraordinary numbers. But to funds collected for sensible purposes

of the Czar perturbed him deeply. As a boy he had met that ill-fated ruler who had visited Gwalior during his Indian tour as Czarevitch. The War seemed to have killed "sedition" in India, but now there was sedition in the West. What use would victory be, if subjects ceased to obey and revere the master set over them by Fate? To his last day Madhav Rao Scindia believed firmly in the Divine Right of Kings.

But despite the work he was doing in connection with the War, the Maharaja was taking a keen interest in the affairs of his State, though he no longer found time for any long tours throughout its length and breadth, and had deliberately curtailed all expenditure even on productive works in order to have more money in hand to assist the British Government in the prosecution of the War.

The agricultural season of 1913-14 had been none too good. In certain parts there had been not merely scarcity but actual famine. Yet the difficulties had been well met. Though countless emigrants had flocked to Malwa from Rajputana, relief had yet been adequate, and the people of Gwalior at least had not been forced to become nomads.

The War too was producing a spurious prosperity. Though the cost of the necessities of life had risen in the towns, so much so that the export of certain commodities had to be controlled, still the peasantry were benefiting by the higher prices for their cotton, wheat, or oil seeds. There had even been a temporary revival of the demand for opium, no longer for export to China but as a pain-killer for army doctors. Even of the State "commercial concerns" some were prospering. The Leather Factory was making money; the State Workshops boring shells as cheaply as any works in India, but still at no loss; the Forest Department supplying unlimited bales of grass for the armies in Egypt and Mesopotamia, even though, under the orders of His Highness, it was providing this fodder either free or at rates which gave little scope for extravagant profits.

The War had put a stop to a mineral survey of the State, but the whole of its territory had been cursorily gone over by competent persons, only for the Darbar to learn that Gwalior as a whole possessed little wealth in the matter of metals or minerals. This was a disappointment to the Maharaja who had another blow when two large dams, designed by Mr. Preston, burst within a day or two of each other. The loss caused to irrigation by the failure of the Tigra Dam, the larger of the two, was very great. The other lake at Sipri had been designed chiefly for pleasure purposes, for the development of Sipri had been going on steadily despite the War. Not a reproach was heard, not a bitter word uttered; the reconstruction of both dams was immediately taken in hand.

But there had been good fortune too. In the first year of the War a daughter had been born to His Highness and in June 1916, the desired son had at last arrived. By Their Gracious Majesties' consent the names of Mary and George were prefixed to Kamla Raja and Jivaji Rao, the Indian names given to the girl and boy, respectively.

In spite of the fact that two out of the four years during which the War lasted were poor from the agricultural point of view and one other distinctly bad, the cultivators as a whole did fairly well thanks to the high prices obtained for such harvests as they reaped. The Maharaja had for some time been considering the introduction of improved agricultural methods and the employment of farm machinery. Owing to the War it was difficult to get scientifically trained experts to start an Agricultural Department, but January 1918 saw its formation with the help of several Americans.

The lines on which His Highness decided to create an interest in scientific agriculture were in many ways his own. Apart from Central Experimental Farms at Lashkar and Ujjain, there was appointed in each district a demonstrator who was given a grant of money from the State and put in charge of a village as *zamindar* or land-holder. He had to maintain a small model farm and to introduce better seed and improved methods of cultivation among the population of the village. When from his profits he had cleared his debts to the State, he was automatically to become a *zamindar* with the same status as an ordinary land-holder.

The successful application of a scheme of this nature turned mainly on the class of personnel employed. Some *zamindars* did well, others badly. The introduction of power-machinery and especially of oil-driven tractors was only a comparative success owing to the fact that the type of machinery best adapted to local conditions was not found at the start.

Here again His Highness wanted results from the first and was inclined to be impatient that they did not come within a twelve-month. His originality was displayed in another method intended to promote the advance of agriculture. A large number of travelling *Upadeshaks* or preachers were trained and entrusted with the duty of touring the villages and addressing the people on the needs of attention to religion, loyalty to the government, sanitation, rural economy, and improved methods of agriculture generally. Despite a certain superficial grounding in the theory of husbandry these lecturers were too weak on the practical side to be of much real use in inducing the cultivator to experiment with new methods. No *Upadeshak* could have made a living by practising what he preached!

The text-book on which the *Upadeshaks* founded their discourses was a fat volume written by His Highness personally. This book "the Zamindar Hitkari," was compiled at spare moments snatched by the Maharaja from his multifarious duties at the time, and large portions of it were written while in the railway train. It was the first of several books of which His Highness was the author and perhaps the most successful. Though much of it and especially the illustrations of power-machinery were completely above the heads of the cultivators, indeed above those of most of the *Upadeshaks*, it contains much teaching of value for the agricultural class for whose benefit it was originally intended.

Not only agriculture but commerce and industry were receiving attention. Various new undertakings, many of which unfortunately had but an ephemeral existence, were started during the war period; but the most ambitious attempt of all was the creation of the Gwalior State Trust. This was a flotation made with State funds at the advice of a London firm of financiers and bankers and was intended to develop trade and manufactures in Gwalior. Of its ill-fated ending more will be said later.

For all that the War was in progress, and each month conditions were becoming more and more difficult, new developments in the State were not hindered. With his many undertakings it had become impossible for His Highness to attempt his usual cold weather tours, but that did not mean that the needs of Gwalior were out of his mind. His State could support a far bigger population than it had. Generously he offered valuable concessions of land to recruits for the Indian Army and hoped thereby, once the War had passed, to attract a large number of new settlers. He had still not abandoned the idea of communication by river with Calcutta. In a note written for the Delhi Sub-Committee appointed to deal with Economic Control and the Regulation of Resources he points out that, as general railway facilities had had to be so curtailed owing to military needs, the British authorities should be requested to co-operate with the Darbar in the construction of river-craft for the navigation of the Chambal. To his death he never gave up finally the idea of the economic possibilities of such river transport in spite of adverse reports and physical difficulties which to other minds were insuperable.

He was seriously perturbed by the spirit of unrest he noticed in the world around him, unrest, that is, among the civil population, and decided on slender premisses that the chief blame must be laid at the door of Education. This he tried to remedy by the issue of new text-books for the primary schools of Gwalior. These readers, in the compilation of which he took much interest, are significant of his general views on educational matters. Written in a pedestrian style which never attains to any literary merit, these text-books try to inculcate utilitarian ideas, thoughts which could be put to practical use, whether in everyday life or in the specialities of agriculture and morals. The diction is of the simplest, the style monotonous and no more elaborate in the fifth reader than in the first, though the ideas expounded in the later readers are more complex than those in the earlier volumes.

The notion that his subjects were growing up with disloyal tendencies seemed to have haunted him at this period, perhaps because of the rebellious attitude of certain of his feudatories whose case as a whole was before the Government of India and who, pending its decision, were taking a pride in flouting the most reasonable expectations of the Darbar behind the shadowy screen of a real or constructive "guarantee."

Such occasional instances of recalcitrancy afforded no real cause for general pessimism to His Highness, for, inspired by his energy and his personality generally, the people of Gwalior were supporting their Ruler nobly in his efforts to help the cause of the Allies. Even the Thakurs, the Rajput landholders in Northern and Central Gwalior, who thirty years before had as a class been openly disaffected towards the Scindia family, were now coming forward with all their resources of men, money, and kind to back up the exertions of their Prince.

This Madhav Rao Scindia recognised and acknowledged in no grudging manner; on many occasions in his speeches or letters he points that for the part Gwalior was playing in the War the credit should go not to himself but to his subjects. And yet the dismal weird he had to dree was the oppressive delusion that the rising generation was growing up full of subversive tendencies, without regard for religion, without respect for their parents and elders, without loyalty to their rulers, and generally possessed by "destructive rather than constructive" ideas.

In actual fact, for all the hardships that the War caused in individual cases, the devotion of the people of Gwalior for their master was blossoming day by day. They had learned that he cared whether they lived or died, whether they were prosperous or poor, happy or miserable; they now rejoiced to see him playing so big a part on a wider stage than Gwalior. They felt they were contemporaries of greatness.

Even in remote Malwa, where in single day's tour it is possible to ride through stray patches of territory belonging to three or four different principalities, the Gwalior peasant was a proud man. The Indore, Bhopal, or Dewas cultivator, if asked of what State he was a subject, would reply of Indore, of Bhopal, or of Dewas as the case might be, but the answer of the Gwalior *ryot* to such a question was always different. He would not say he was a Gwalior man, in fact he might refuse to admit it. His reply would invariably be the same. He was the man of Madhav Maharaj. Subconsciously he felt that he had gained in personal dignity and honour by having such a Chief as his Ruler.

In the reviews written as introductions to the annual Administration Reports during the War, His Highness had continued to find little right with the work of the members of his government or of the heads of departments under them; and yet such fault-finding was at this period recognised generally to be the outcome of no personal resentment on their master's part. Though many of his officers were very seriously overworked, the Maharaja was toiling harder than any of them.

Even if results were expected almost before some new line of policy had had time to come into full operation, they knew that such an impossible expectation was due mainly to a passionate longing that the Gwalior State should by superhuman efforts prove itself able to give more effective support in hastening the conclusion of the War.

During the year 1918 it was commonly observed that the Maharaja's health which for a time had seemed much better was failing again, though his energy showed no signs of faltering. On several occasions he was laid up with fever and once during the monsoon at Sipri developed a boil on his neck which it was feared might turn into a carbuncle. During these periods of confinement to bed he would grow very annoyed with the doctors who could not cure him in a day and might perhaps refuse to take their medicines, but, even in bed with a temperature, he would be busy giving orders about some necessary work or discussing some new line of policy to be adopted forthwith.

The announcement of the Armistice came almost as suddenly as the Declaration of War in 1914. From Sipri, or Shivpuri as the town had recently been renamed, His Highness motored down to Lashkar and from the steps of the General Post Office made an impromptu speech to a mass meeting of the citizens of his capital, a speech that was perhaps the most impressive feat of oratory of his life.

In a stentorian voice which for all its volume was modulated by the unconscious artistry of genuine sentiment Madhav Rao Scindia proclaimed his devotion to the King-Emperor. Loyalty to the British Crown was the guiding principle of all his acts, the only justification for his position as a Ruler; it was the right by which he claimed allegiance from his subjects and the touchstone by which the people of Gwalior should test all their public actions. In such loyalty there was no place for self-seeking motives nor for interested policy.

For the treasure and resources of the State which had been so lavishly expended during the war he had only been the appointed trustee of his subjects. It was their fidelity that he had striven to vindicate. For himself he made no claim; he had acted merely as he would act so long as life lasted, true to the principles he had announced thirteen years before. He would aim at securing the stability of the British Empire.

That this speech in its entirety was never properly taken down at the time is a misfortune that must for ever be deplored, but in any case no written words could convey an adequate expression of the passion which genuine sentiment imported to his tones. As he spoke that day even the dullest of his listeners recognised that he was not merely big. For the moment at least he was great.

It is possible that, if the cynical personage who had opined Scindia to be "the most seditious chief in India" had been present as a listener among the attentive masses in the city square, he might have been convinced of the falsity of his estimate, assuming that he had ever really voiced it.

For the Maharaja the day ended with an irritating anti-climax. Fever attacked him and he grew impatient with his physician who could not bring down a high temperature to normal by a single dose of medicine. Except for "Guruji," all the doctors he had known were humbugs!

CHAPTER VIII.

1919–1925

THE sudden termination of the Great War came to Gwalior as a wonderful relief. The seasons had been none too favourable for the crops, and the drain on the food resources of the State had emptied the villages of their usual stores of grain, kept as a reserve for seed and scarcity emergencies. Though there had been no actual famine since the year 1913-14, the prices of food stuffs were still at famine level and were telling very hardly on the dwellers in the towns and on all those in receipt of fixed wages. In India where rates of pay rest not only on direct economic factors but on custom, the "lag" between rising prices and rising wages is always prone to be unduly emphasised.

Yet in Gwalior, as in the territories of the Allies as a whole, men were possessed by the delusion that at last the millennium would be theirs for the asking and that heaven would come true on earth without the need of dying for it. A great industrial boon was anticipated for the world at large, and Gwalior must share in it. To this end it was not enough, thought His Highness, to rely on private initiative or on the various industries just then being madly pioneered by the Gwalior State Trust. An Economic Development Board was formed for the advance and co-ordination of commercial and industrial activities generally. The main ideas underlying the creation of this advisory and consultative body were sound. In addition to local talent, the Board had the advantage of the assistance of prominent business men from British India who accepted seats on it at the invitation of His Highness.

Decorations and other rewards were bestowed by the Government of India and by the Darbar on various subjects of the State whose work in the War had been meritorious. To His Highness personally had already come the honour of a G. B. E. and the distinction of his salute raised permanently to twenty-one guns as well as his advancement to the rank of Lieutenant-General in the British Army.

Gradually the Imperial Service Troops were drafted back from overseas, life became more normal, and generally the State seemed likely to enjoy the piping times of peace. That the industrial boon quickly petered out affected the State but little; that, thanks to gross mismanagement and culpable neglect, if to nothing worse, on the part of those whom His Highness had so implicitly trusted against advice, the Gwalior State Trust was quickly to lose or waste the large sums placed at its disposal was a blow to his personal pride, though the actual money squandered in no way cramped the administration of the State. So far as Gwalior was concerned the next quinquennium was to be a miserable time for another reason. Whatever may be said for or against a personal Government, it is a fact that, if an autocrat has the feeling of his people behind him, that people inevitably shares his joys and sorrows. It quickly became a matter of general knowledge, indeed a fact visible to all, that Madhav Maharaj was unhappy.

His troubles were many. The most intimate was the failing health of his mother. It had been a justifiable excuse for the declining two invitations to attend Imperial Conferences. It was now a very cogent reason against an immediate visit to England, such as it had been generally anticipated, would be one of the first post-war actions of His Highness.

There were other worries, mainly of a political nature. The long-drawn-out case of the "guaranteed estates" had not as yet been decided by the Government of India. The two cantonments of the Central India Horse at Goona and Agar continued still to be the irritation that they had been for years. Above all there was the spirit of unrest that His Highness saw spreading around him in British India.

In an article "India Loquitur" written for the *Times of India* "the Maharaja had given his views on government, indeed his justification for personal rule, in the guise of a reasoned statement as to what would make for the prosperity of India as a whole, but so far as he could judge the inhabitants of British India had lost their heads and would not listen to sense as he visioned it. Everywhere the cry was for *Swaraj* and His Highness could not believe that Jack was as good as his master. Even if he were, he had no right to try to prove or disprove it by revolutionary methods or even by passive resistance. Both were destructive rather than constructive.

To him it seemed that the root of the trouble lay in a wrong system of education. If the scheme of education were reformed, all would be well, but a reformation of the system meant a reformation of the teaching *personnel*, and that could not be arranged in a day. He fretted that education could not show quick results.

The death of his mother the Dowager Maharani in September 1919 was a great shock. The love between mother and son had always been very real. Her sympathy had ever been able to soothe his nerves when tattered by over-work or ill-health. While never attempting to interfere in any way in the administration, her kind heart had suggested many gracious acts for her son to carry out.

In connection with the passing of his mother may be mentioned an incident which admirably illustrates the simplicity of the Maharaja's nature—his deep convictions, such as they were, or, as the scoffer would say, his puerile and superstitious credulity.

When the end of "Jija Maharaj" was near, he strove to propitiate the gods and goddesses, he besought them to spare her life. He invoked their mercy through the prayers of the needy and the suffering, and for this purpose he had brought to her bedside seventy-five thousand rupees in silver. Her limp hand was made to touch the pile, which then went out to relieve the distress of the indigent. The gods were inexorable—his mother died. In the simplicity of his heart the Maharaja wailed "I gave a fortune in charity to make my mother live. Still she died!"

Her death occurred at Shivpuri (Sipri) which was now showing the results of the care His Highness had been lavishing on its development. Her mausoleum placed at one end of the park is a beautiful building, near which to-day is rising the marble cenotaph of her son.

The Maharaja needed rest. Perhaps at last he would recognise the need which so many of his friends had long impressed on him, despite the fact that their insistence evoked his scorn. A visit to England would do him good! How could he let go the helm when times were so out of joint? Others might take leave if they liked, if they were too lazy to work. How could he get away just at the moment? Conditions in India were getting worse, not better. Perhaps in the next year he would make a trip to Europe. Meanwhile his health was his own concern. It was a subject on which he had not asked advice. That was enough. He had been born in Gwalior. He must die in Gwalior.

High prices were causing trouble especially amongst the people of the Karera district in Central Gwalior. Dacoity which had flourished in that tract in the bad old days had been scotched years before, but now it was again raising its head. The district was a troublesome one; not very rich agriculturally, nor provided with many roads, since much of it was jungle, and in any case difficult to control from its scattered nature and the close proximity of British India and the inept jurisdictions of various petty States.

The police seemed powerless. Like man-eating tigers the dacoits would make one "kill" in the Darbar's territories and the next in the Jhansi or Lalitpur Districts of the United Provinces; the third might be in some other State, such as Datia. But in any case the majority of the dacoits were by common consent agreed to be Gwalior men.

What happened may be told in the words of a nameless writer who has composed the preface to the fourth published volume of His Highness' speeches.

"Dacoity was rife in the Narwar District of which the worst affected area was the Karera Pargana. Reports of crime came in with painful frequency and the descriptions of dacoits' excesses made one's hair stand on end. The British representative accredited to the Gwalior Court was bursting with suppressed rage and would hardly conceal his avidity to flame forth into righteous pyrotechnics; the men about court writhed in unspoken agony or at best talked with bated breath about the immobility of the Darbar in the face of such a public scandal! And yet no punitive force was mobilised nor even the Pargana's Police strength augmented! All this while the Maharaja, perfectly unperturbed by the happenings, was giving the long rope to the stricken district. Six months passed, but no gesture was forthcoming of any contemplated relief to the suffering poor."

"Came March, 1921, and then the Maharaja published far and wide over the district his esoteric conviction that organised dacoity could not flourish in any part of the country without the connivance, and, indeed, the active, though clandestine, participation of the *zamindars* of the locality. The dacoits must be the *zamindars* themselves or their near relatives, and they could not subsist and maraud without being rationed by accomplices. Therefore, summarily, he gave them a month's notice to bring the dacoits into

Karera on the date fixed when personally he would be there. If they failed, it would be the worse for them, and all the might of the State would be bent upon their indiscriminate extirpation."

"At dead of night, preceding the appointed day, unarmed and unescorted except for the driver and one companion, the Maharaja leisurely motored to Karera: expecting not surprises or reprisals but to meet some of the desperadoes quietly wending their way to the tryst. The journey proved uneventful because the Maharaja had already been preceded to Karera by many of the malefactors. Morning dawned and a goodly contingent had assembled. Another twenty-four hours and the muster reached the desired total of 120 dacoits."

"On the second morning at 10 o'clock there was a Darbar at which the assembled *zamindars* were addressed—several hundred in number. No pardons had been previously promised and no judicial trials were ordered."

"The *zamindars* gathered were called upon to determine individual enormity and to propose sentences. Thus a situation was created in which neither grudge nor nepotism could retain a foothold. The aggrieved and the suffering were all there, to call on and to identify. The sentences were proposed, and the Maharaja, in the exercise of his prerogative, straightway confirmed them.

No dacoit escaped the punishment which his deserts merited, hanging, long term imprisonment, forfeiture of property. Thus did the Maharaja meet an ugly situation and challenged the votaries of judicial niceties who live and move have their being in the mazes of adjective and substantive law, in meticulous procedure and stale exactitudes, to judge between him-and Justice."

His Highness motored back to Lashkar satisfied with his work. Not yet had he lost grip.

In May he took leave for two months! Handing over the charge of the State with all formality to the Senior Maharani and two councillors as her advisers, he went into British India for a holiday. His vacation was spent in watching the growth of general unrest and in working off the arrears of some special files he had taken with him for leisurely disposal!

He returned with the idea that most of his officers were suffering from "sleeping sickness," and that "degree holders talk too much and so do their certificates and testimonials." His general health was certainly worse than it had been before he had left Gwalior, but he would take no advice on that subject. He was far more interested in the latest improvements in course of completion at Shivpuri.

His introductory review to the annual Administration Report is full of blistering scorn and complaints at the small amount of progress made. It was because the work already accomplished in Gwalior was so much the result of his own personal efforts that he found little satisfaction in what already achieved for his State. His virile mind could never look backwards. Any progress made he could hardly see, since he compared existing conditions not with a less satisfactory past but with a future ideal set before his vision, an ideal alas! that, as his health weakened, seemed to him to be withdrawing further and further from his eager grasp.

On insufficient premisses he had decided that his officers were not anxious to give effect to the plans he had formed for each State department.

"But there it is again; the same old story that I cannot be everywhere to drive the people to carry out my instructions. If I do too much, then I know people get disgusted with me. If I do not, then I see that instructions are not carried out. No one has realised the position of an administrator, nor are people prepared nowadays to see to reason. Still I do not mind what people think. I feel that I must do my duty."

Such is a very typical extract from his review of an Administration Report at this period in which confidential memoranda, scarifying the work of various departments, appeared continually. Results were not coming in quickly enough. If his officers and subjects were not producing the desired results with the speed anticipated, it could only be because they were not so eager for them as their Ruler was. And not to be so eager was equivalent to being disloyal. He was beginning to suspect even where he trusted. His innate nobility of spirit told him that such suspicions were unjust, were unworthy of him, and so he trusted all the more. Yet he could not rid his mind of the impression that his nobles, his officials, and his subjects generally were actively or passively desirous of obstructing progress.

That was the real tragedy of his latter days, a tragedy compared to which pales into insignificance the disaster of his death in a foreign land far away from the people of Gwalior whose welfare had been the beacon by which he had steered his Ship of State.

For trust had begotten trust. His earliest reforms had been regarded with apathy or hostility; but the worth of those new practices had been proved by time, and enthusiastically his subjects had begun to follow Scindia's star. Gladly they were marching along behind the master set over them by Fate, instead of needing to be dragged on by force against their personal inclinations, as had been the case during the first two decades of his rule. From a dull acquiescence in their Prince's will, his whims as they had regarded them, Sardar and *ryot*, rich man and poor, all were daily growing in political stature and wisdom. They were getting to be proud that they had a stake in Gwalior, which from a number of scattered patches of territory

Madhav Rao Scindia had forged into a real political entity. A sense of deep loyalty to him pervaded their hearts, far deeper and truer than that given to any of his ancestors.

This was the position; but the spell now cast on the Maharaja, decreed that once true devotion had come to him he could not recognise it, well as he had earned it. He stuck to his work for his people but that work was no longer a joy to him. Nor was it a weariness exactly, for all that his inability to make up his tired mind on some simple subject would cause a distressingly common repetition on his files of such orders as "What does Majlis (*i. e.*, the Council) think of this?" or "Put up next Sipri Season." Work had been the habit of years. It now became almost a dope which blunted the haunting fear that the world, as he wanted it, could never be built, indeed was falling to pieces all around him.

Here was not obsession but mental obfuscation, a delusion battening on a broken constitution; but he could not realise the truth and would listen to no arguments against so false a conclusion. Courageous to the last, he determined to fight what he considered were the subversive tendencies gathering force on every side. His word was still law. He would, so far at least as Gwalior was concerned, attempt to bind posterity, an undertaking the futility of which he would a decade earlier have been the first to recognise.

Perhaps to the last he was aware of its impossibility, but in any case he felt it his duty to essay the task, vain though it might be.

"The Darbar Policy" with its twelve volumes, to the compilation of which the Maharaja devoted so much time and labour, is admittedly a very uneven piece of work. It contains a great deal of unnecessary repetition and occasionally apparent, indeed real, contradictions. Certain of the author's own administrative acts after its publication ran counter to the policy he had himself laid down in it! Unfortunately too the book would give any casual reader who had never met His Highness no proper idea of the commanding personality of the writer. In it side by side with shrewd criticisms and suggestions or lucid, if unconventional, hints on statecraft, are to be found undignified cavillings at such necessary people as doctors, lawyers, engineers, and university graduates. It displays little sense of humour, that outward and visible sign of health and of a sense of proportion which had once characterised Scindia above any Indian Prince of his time.

Yet admitting its manifold imperfections, the "Darbar Policy" is a work to be reckoned with seriously in Gwalior at all events, if only because the obvious earnestness of its writer pervades its every page. The times are out of joint, but in Scindia's realm at any cost arrangements must be made for such continuity of policy that any work so far done be taken as a basis on which to rest future achievement. Whatever the future may yield, the best of the old must be retained, so that on it may be raised a stately structure perfect in all its parts and a credit to the builder. It was for this object that the Maharaja would sometimes toil at this book for eight hours of daylight and then again continue his labours at night when sleep was denied him. For years he had slept badly.

In certain passages can be read the author's impatience that the hours of day are not forty-eight, occasionally too perhaps his premonition of an early release from the "bonds" of flesh. The compilation of this great work gave the writer the comfort of feeling that no thread of government had as yet slipped from his fingers; its completion afforded him a temporary sense of satisfaction. He knew that the book was no great literary effort, but he had vindicated his views, and the world must see that he was right. He had done his duty and laid down a definite policy by which each department of the Gwalior State could check its work.

But all the people in Gwalior would not read this book. Yet they must know and understand his policy. Perhaps it was this idea which led him in 1921 to create the Majlis-i-Am or general assembly, as members of which selected representatives from each district of the State were summoned to attend. To this body, though its functions were purely advisory, was entrusted the consideration of many subjects closely concerned with the public weal. The Maharaja's personality was ever far more effective than his written words. He would explain and justify his aims by speeches delivered to the members of this popular assembly.

About this time the Government of India at long last settled the question of the "guaranteed estates" and tardily admitted the justice of the Darbar's claim. First and last the matter had taken twelve years for decision and, now that it was finished, it gave Scindia little joy. He was more gratified by the Gwalior Residency being placed in direct touch with the Political Department of the Government of India. The delay in the settlement of the "guarantee" case he had attributed chiefly to the unexpeditious methods adopted by the office of the Agent to the Governor-General at Indore. Now at least Gwalior had regained its old status of immediate communication through its Resident with the Supreme Power.

For many years the State had ceased to look towards the Deccan, but a strong community feeling, increased by the prominent part they had played in the War, was stirring among the Marathas in India generally. The Marathas of the Deccan had begun to feel a pride in their kinsfolk of Central India and Guzerat where the greatest of present-day Maratha Chiefs held sway.

The cenotaph at Wanowrie near Poona to the memory of the great Mahadji Scindia, erected by His Highness some years before, had attracted considerable attention among Marathas generally. For political reasons a wide, if pretended, interest was being manifested by the Swarajists in Shivaji, the Maratha hero, who had delivered his countrymen from the thrall of the Mughal Emperors. For all practical purposes the Swarajists may be held to have commandeered the memory of this great man for their own ends.

A memorial in honour of Shivaji was to be erected. To this proposal His Highness had no objection, though he had a deep-rooted aversion to the spirit behind the movement. He held out against the communal aspect of the proposal and refused to join the movement until it was agreed that the memorial should become an Indian and national undertaking. If Shivaji's name was to be commemorated because he was really a great man, then he must be treated as a national hero and his greatness emphasised by its practical acknowledgment. All India must join in doing honour to a great Indian. All India must subscribe to the memorial and the management of the institution must be representative of all communities.

In May, 1921, a Maratha Conference was held at Gwalior attended by representatives of that community throughout all India. In November of the same year, thanks largely to His Highness' influence and to the efforts of the Maharaja of Kolhapur, the foundation stone of the Shri Shivaji Memorial was laid at Poona by His Royal Highness the Prince of Wales! The Gwalior Lancers, commanded by Madhav Rao Scindia in person, formed part of the escort of His Royal Highness, but even more interesting to the spectators was the sight of irregular horsemen of Gwalior and Kolhapur in their ancient Maratha uniforms lining the street and looking as if for the moment they were once more the swaggering masters of Poona that they had been in the days of the great Mahadji. In Poona there were no disturbances such as had marred the arrival of His Royal Highness in Bombay.

February 1922 witnessed a four-day visit of the Prince of Wales to Gwalior, this being the third occasion on which the Jai Bilas Palace had been honoured by the presence of an Heir to the British Crown.

His Royal Highness in his speech at the State Banquet made a special reference to the Maharaja's work in the Chamber of Princes and on the Princes' Committee, of which bodies from their inauguration Scindia had been as energetic a member as any Chief in

India, as well as being the most important Prince of any Indian State who had regularly attended the meetings of the Chamber.

Perhaps the most prominent part the Maharaja ever played in the deliberations of this body was in the year 1923. For some time many newspapers had gone out of their way to vilify the administrations of various Native States, in the existence of which they saw perhaps the strongest bulwark against the wilder excesses of *Swaraj.* It was proposed to protect the Princes against such a misuse of the powers of journalism. In the debate that ensued His Highness took a very strong line. He did not want any protection, he could not see how any Chief needed such defence, provided he was doing his duty by his subjects. A Ruler should be prepared to have his acts revealed in the bright glare of publicity. It was a plucky speech, such as its speaker might have delivered a decade before. For the moment, in spite of his wasted frame, his hearers were able to forget that the Scindia who now spoke retained but a shadow of his former physical and intellectual strength. At that instant he towered above his princely colleagues and was his old self once more.

His own methods of treating press criticism were quite original. If some administrative measure of his was questioned in the Press, he would summon to Gwalior from British India the editor of the paper that had criticised his act, put all his cards on the table, show his guest the files relating to the subject, and then demand that, with all the facts before him, the newspaper man should suggest some alternative and better line of action or policy.

In such encounters he always came off the victor. It is in reference to such occasions that in one of his reviews on the administration of the State occur the words:—"My friends the newspapers start shelling with Machine-guns on subjects which they know nothing about and of which they have no experience as actual administrators."

But from all the successes that came his way in the years 1923 and 1924 he drew little satisfaction, for his physical health was failing rapidly. Refusing all rest, he sat at his files as usual, unless his ill health actually forced him to stay in his bed. Even when thus immobilised, he would have his sickroom filled with officers, with whom he would discuss some reforms that must be hurried on or new schemes which he held were for the welfare of the State.

Certain of his projects were meeting with little success; for example, the *Upadeshaks* or travelling lecturers were doing no real good, but he had grown impatient of any criticism and thought that any suggestion to the effect that this particular scheme had failed merely meant that his officers wanted to thwart the project just because it had been and still was a favourite idea of his own! The only source of failure was, in his opinion, that the *Upadeshaks* were not sufficiently numerous; so their number must be increased. He could not see that the ordinary travelling lecturer had not his own vivid personality, which alone might have imparted life to the printed instructions given in the "Zamindar Hitkari" that he had written for his people's good.

In his administrative acts he was daily becoming more autocratic, not because he loved absolutism, but because a subconscious instinct told him that his grip on affairs of State was rapidly loosening. He must not relax effort; he must assert himself.

He would criticise, where once he would have praised, for fear that his officers might grow to be conceited and lose all sense of discipline! Those same officers, from real feelings of loyalty, were often hard put to it to conceal from the world at large the fact, patent to all his intimate friends, that the Maharaja was no longer equal physically or mentally to deal with the innumerable administrative matters which he still insisted on handling.

As each spring season came, he would postpone to the next year the holiday in Europe that he had agreed to take. In India the wave of unrest appeared to be ebbing. The Maharaja saw this himself, but he would not admit the fact. He seemed to think that the idea of getting him to spend a few months away from his work was a deep laid scheme to hinder the progress of State affairs!

During 1924 there was no single month in which he did not have to take to his bed for a few days or more. His powerful frame had become emaciated; his clothes sagged about him. It was mere vitality, if that be distinguishable from an effort of the will, not physical strength, that enabled him to do anything at all. In vain did his physicians try to persuade him to adopt a regular diet or to take the medicines they prescribed. The idea of doctors was only to keep their patient in bed so that they could show what great men they were! Such was his common retort to their entreaties.

In the spring of 1925 came an invitation from His Most Gracious Majesty the King-Emperor, for His Highness to visit England that summer. With the progress of his malady the Maharaja had grown more and more superstitious. The preceding twelvemonth had to him been full of evil omens. One of the emblems of the Mahi-Maratib, the high decoration given to his ancestors by the Mughal Emperor at Delhi, had been broken by accident; a big gun had run away with the elephant which was hauling it up the steep incline of the Gwalior Fortress and the huge beast had been hurled over a parapet to meet its death by a fall down a precipice; at the last Mohurram festival either lightning or a stray spark had ignited the covering beneath which the Maharaja's *tazia* had rested and in a few minutes both covering and *tazia* had been reduced to ashes. Such a trio of ill-starred portents had never occurred in Gwalior since the day of his accession.

But whatever might be ahead of him, Madhav Rao Scindia was now steadfast in his intention. His Majesty had summoned him. There could be no question of a vassal not obeying the smallest wish of his liege lord. He was happy to have had his mind thus made up for him.

Handing over the charge of the State to the Senior Maharani he sailed in April for Europe.

He was in great physical pain, for on starting he had a large boil on his neck which he had refused to have lanced. During the voyage he still obstinately declined to have it treated properly, for its excision would have demanded chloroform. The boil had by this time shown itself as a definite carbuncle.

On arrival at Marseilles his health forbade any immediate continuation of his journey. With the assistance of a Paris physician, he was after a few days removed to the French capital, where much against his will an operation was performed by one of the most famous of French surgeons now living. The operation was completely successful, and all was going well. The Maharaja was removed from a hotel in the centre of the city to the Château de Madrid on the outskirts of the Bois de Boulogne. He was making steady progress to recovery when suddenly he assumed a recalcitrant air and refused to have his wound dressed regularly. He objected to the masterful manner in which, to save his life, the French doctors insisted on treating his case. Unknown to his friends, he had cabled to Bombay for the despatch of a *hakim* who had on several occasions treated him for minor ailments, such as boils of an unimportant nature.

His friends, his officers, all besought him to listen to reason and to allow his wound to be dressed properly, but he turned a deaf ear to all their entreaties. In consequence the wound grew steadily worse, and another operation became necessary. Lord Dawson of Penn, the King's physician, who had been summoned from London succeeded after much persuasion in getting him to consent. In this matter the doctor was ably seconded by His Highness the Gaekwar of Baroda whose presence in Paris at this time was invaluable. While the Gaekwar was in the sickroom, the invalid would generally suffer his wound to be dressed and would take his medicine. With infinite patience the Gaekwar would spend hours by the Maharaja's side.

The second operation, a very serious one, was skilfully carried out by the great French Surgeon, and the Maharaja, after a few anxious days, again seemed on the high road to recovery.

His two children and their mother had arrived a few days before, and the danger to his life seemed to have passed. Though weak and taking little nourishment but many cigarettes, His Highness was undoubtedly in a less critical condition than he had been. Hopes of his recovery were very high.

Then the *hakim* arrived from Bombay. Immediately the Maharaja insisted on a change of treatment. The physicians who had attended him so far and so well had to be dismissed much to the sorrow of all his friends.

After two days of the *hakim's* treatment the wound became unhealthy; the patient's temperature rose. His condition had grown toxic.

The second floor of the Château de Madrid which in its entirety had been given over for the occupation of His Highness and his suite became a gloomy place filled with grave faces, lowered voices, and dire forebodings. Those present felt that they hated the hotel, to the gardens of which each afternoon and evening the *élite* of Paris would flock for tea and after-dinner dances. In his room lay the Maharaja almost too weak to move, and with the remnant of his strength rapidly failing: yet without intermission he kept smoking one cigarette after another. Gratified at having forced a change of treatment in his case, he became suddenly content and affirmed that now he would soon recover.

Even the *hakim* had to admit that his ointments were proving inefficacious, and so at the last moment a desperate effort was made to resort to saner methods of cure.

It was too late. About ten minutes to four on the afternoon of the 5th of June, 1925, His Highness asked for a cigarette. Presently he seemed to fall asleep, and the cigarette went out. One of the watchers took it from the lifeless fingers. He recognised, as did all in the room, that the string of the kite of Madhav Rao Scindia's soul had been cut. His spirit had soared into the unknown.

It had just struck four. On the second floor of the Château de Madrid arose piteous wailing. Below from the garden at the back of the hotel came the clash of the jazz music for the foxtrot with the daily *thé dansant* was as usual opening.

CHAPTER IX.

SCINDIA AS A SOLDIER AND SPORTSMAN.

THE dictum of Machiavelli that War ought to be the only study of a Prince would never have been accepted by Madhav Rao Scindia. In his eyes soldiering was but one of many activities in which a Ruler should show himself proficient. While his army was to him a never failing source of interest, a part of the State's organization to which he devoted the deepest attention, he was yet by general consent less of a born soldier than his father.

In his view, maybe a correct view, an army was no mere weapon of offence or defence; it was to be an ever open school of discipline. The training in discipline, which is essential to the creation of an efficient soldier, was in itself a sufficient justification for the large proportion of the revenue which the Military Department absorbed, apart from any consideration of the practical purpose that a body of troops might serve.

The late Maharaja, however, if no born soldier, was certainly a made soldier, perhaps largely a self-made soldier. From his youth he had received a sound grounding in drill, to the details of which he devoted himself with the application he always gave to any

subject that roused his interest. He was drilled himself, he drilled others. From an early age he was able to take charge of any regiment or of a brigade and put it through a useful day's work in the field. But, unlike his father, he had found other absorbing occupations during his minority and in the first few years after his investiture, and so he was not content to confine his activities to parades and field-days as Jayaji Rao had done in his youth.

The internal economy of his troops never failed to receive from Madhav Rao Scindia its due attention; and this side of his army's life was one that on the receipt of his powers he found to have been much neglected. Although the barracks, vacated by the British brigade in 1886 on the rendition to the State of the Morar Cantonment, afforded good accommodation for some regiments, a large proportion of the Gwalior troops were very poorly quartered and little real attention was paid to their health and general well-being. Provided the turn-out on parade was smart and the ceremonial march past all that it should be, the conditions under which the soldiers lived were not considered a matter of supreme importance at the time when His Highness assumed control of the State.

From the first this defect received the Maharaja's most careful consideration, and during the three decades of his rule, steady, though not showy, progress was made in the matter of improved lines and barrack accommodation generally. To-day the troops are as a whole very well housed and found.

In his army, as it came to him at his accession, graft and nepotism were common. That such a state of affairs has now completely disappeared is due to the insistence of His Highness on honesty and efficiency as the first qualification for commissioned rank.

Thirty years ago Scindia's Army was enlisted largely from outside the boundaries of the State, and this in spite of the fact that several of the northern districts of Gwalior provided certain regiments of the Indian Army with recruits of a very suitable type. That at present the majority of the State troops are drawn from within the limits of Gwalior is in the main the result of the wise policy of His Highness who recognised the necessity for recruitment from a class with a stake in Gwalior.

Though the Maharaja on one occasion accompanied his Transport Corps to its base during the Tirah Expedition in 1896, the only real active service he ever saw was in the autumn of 1900, when he proceeded to China where he was attached to the staff of General Gaselee. Much as he enjoyed the experience, he would, in discussing his adventures during the Boxer Rising, regretfully complain that he was not allowed to go to China until most of the serious fighting was over.

That on one occasion he had been entrusted with the carrying of despatches and that, while he was travelling by river-craft, his boat came under hostile fire were not particularly exciting experiences. If ever he went on field service again, he did not want a staff appointment; any post even in the non-commissioned ranks would suit him, provided it gave him some work to do, work of which his energy could make a success. This at any rate he affirmed, and in making such a statement His Highness was quite sincere. While in uniform, he could obey as well as command. During his earlier years, before he was stricken by diabetes, he could endure hardships as well as any man, and at no time was he at all solicitous about his personal comfort. When tired out during a tour, or on a *shikar* expedition, or at army manœuvres, he would throw himself on the ground and sleep without the need of mattress, pillow, or blanket.

The original offer of two Imperial Service Cavalry regiments and a transport corps made to the Indian Government during his minority was an action of the Council of Regency of which he had highly approved. Without being asked, he in 1904 increased the quota of his Imperial Service Troops, as already stated, by a third regiment of cavalry, two infantry battalions, and an addition to his transport of one hundred carts.

But though, thanks to their superior training and equipment and arms, the Imperial Service Troops of the

State were far more efficient than the rest of his Army, than, that is to say, the so-called "local troops," their duties being confined to internal defence, the Maharaja always objected most strongly to any distinction being made between the two classes of soldiers. Both, as part of Scindia's Army, he claimed, deserved the same treatment; for were not both maintained not for the honour and glory of the State and its Ruler but to assist the Empire in any emergency? Such was his frequent contention.

Slighting remarks about the "local troops" by tactless inspecting officers of the Imperial Service Regiments often caused His Highness considerable annoyance. So far as he was personally concerned, he treated every man-at-arms, whether a trooper from an Imperial Service Lancer Regiment or one of his irregular cavalry, in exactly the same way and at manœuvres would take a special pride in taking under his command some of the less efficient of his corps.

Each year a month or more was devoted to manœuvres, and this was always a most strenuous time. His Highness would stay in camp throughout the month and live the same life as his troops. During this period the army got little rest as the twenty-four hours were filled with work, general training, field days, or night attacks. After a heavy day would follow a lecture which officers had to attend, and it would be late before they could retire to rest, possibly to be awakened after an hour or two's sleep by a night alarm or occasionally by some practical joke worked on a large scale.

At such manœuvres not only all the troops at the capital, but also those at the Karera and Ujjain Cantonments were called into requisition, even the bullock batteries with the bullocks' "humps dressed to a nicety" or the clumsy elephant batteries, which were a greater success as picturesque survivals at a review parade than useful even in mock warfare.

In his earlier years the Maharaja was a constant student of the War Game, in playing which all his senior officers had to take a part. He was an excellent map-reader, had a fair eye for country, and possessed a detailed knowledge of Field Service Regulations and the drill books of the three arms (though on occasion he was too prone to try to improve on those drill books) and generally could hold his own against any of his officers in tactics or strategy.

At camps of exercise he insisted on the attendance of those of his officers who had been given honorary military rank in his army, even if they were civilians by nature and upbringing. He maintained that such an outing did them good, as indeed was probably the case: yet this annual interlude in their normal lives was no holiday. After their military duties for the day were over, they had by lantern-light to deal with their office files and generally to keep their administrative work up-to-date. If they found such a life under canvas no leisurely one, they yet could comfort themselves with the reflection that it was the same life that their master was then leading; for like themselves he would be working by lamp-light through his usual pile of office work which daily was sent out to his camp from the palace. Indeed occasionally the Maharaja would during manœuvres arrange all the details of some new reform he was introducing into the civil administration, and do this without neglecting his ordinary office files, since he insisted that the free life in camp enabled his brain to be more active and so to cope with a larger volume of work!

While he greatly valued his appointment as A. D. C. to the King-Emperor, Madhav Rao Scindia never set much store by the various honorary ranks in the British Army which were conferred on him at different times. For example, on his elevation to the rank of Major-General, he is reported to have said that he would have far preferred the gift to his army of a single battery of comparatively modern pieces of artillery. His patience was sorely tried by the realisation that none of his guns possessed any military value, and that they could not throw a cannon ball a quarter of a mile with any accuracy. Such as they were, his batteries were admirably horsed with strong Walers, the tackle all it should be, the drivers and gunners as well trained as their antiquated ordnance would allow: but, and this was his incessant complaint, the situation was ludicrous. Not merely were the guns years behind the times, but as each twelvemonth passed, they were growing less and less effective by the mere lapse of time.

Once encouraged by the easy assurance of a somewhat flamboyant Military Secretary to a Commander-in-Chief, Scindia applied for more modern armament for his batteries, as he had done on several previous occasions from 1895 onwards. After considerable discussion the new guns arrived. They were parked on an open space near the Jai Bilas Palace, and Scindia came out to look at them, hurrying along with his characteristic short strides.

A glance sufficed. These were no modern weapons. They were the same smooth-bore, muzzle-loading guns that he had already, though possibly cast a year or two later than the cannon with which his artillery was then armed; but at least just as useless so far as the latest battery training was concerned. He walked away without a word.

To a Political Officer who said that nothing better should have been expected, for, if one Indian Prince were given modern guns, all the rest would clamour for them, Scindia put his case forcibly. Why, he asked, could not the Supreme Government discriminate between Chiefs who from motives of loyalty wanted to make their armies efficient and those who only used their artillery for firing salutes?

The reply of the Political Officer is not on record. Possibly he had not grasped the fact that loyalty to the British Crown was an article of faith which Madhav Rao Scindia had inherited from his father and which he had developed into a personal religion. At the time he was striving to make his irregular troops more efficient and was merely derided for his pains. What was the good of wasting time on them? Such was the common criticism by outsiders who occasionally came to Gwalior. Did Scindia think that they or indeed any of his troops would be of the slightest use in an emergency?

Criticism of this sort would cause him the greatest annoyance, even more irritation than the unworthy suspicion, voiced in certain quarters by unimaginative persons, that his object in putting some of his irregular horse into khaki, in training them in accordance with the cavalry drill books, and in supplying them with some antiquated type of blunderbuss in addition to the sabres they already carried was to create an army of such size and efficiency as might be an embarrassment to the Indian Army in time of war!

Even if such critics still held the views of the servants of John Company a century before, Scindia's own ideas had moved with the times. Loyalty to the British connection was a passion with him as it had been with his father, whom absurd rumours had once credited with the wish of passing all the adult population of Gwalior through a course of military training; of whose army a famous war correspondent after watching what he admitted to be a very creditable display of tactics concluded his description with the question "*mais à quoi bon*"?

Its greatest detractors had to admit that, during the Great War, Scindia's Army not merely proved no embarrassment to the British Forces in India, but was of a considerable assistance to the Allies in various parts of the world.

After that struggle was over it was decided that the forces of the Indian States should be re-organised. A Committee after careful consideration sent in a report that in future such armies should be divided into A, B, and C class troops. The A class troops were to be trained and armed exactly on the same scale as regiments in the Indian Army; B class troops were to be a second line; and C class nothing much more than armed police.

The proposal, involving a considerably increased expenditure on the armies of those States, which adopted the scheme, postulated too that more modern artillery was to be supplied to these "State Forces" as they were to be called.

The Maharaja was delighted. He would willingly meet all the additional costs of the proposed reorganisation, for at last he would get some breech-loading guns which, if of a type just being discarded by the British Army, were at least of some military value.

The scheme went to England for sanction. Thanks, rumour says, to the views of an elderly gentleman at the India Office, the proposal, as finally approved, did not include the provision for any new ordnance. Scindia stuck to, and out for, his guns. If the scheme were not sanctioned *in toto*, then he did not want the new rifles allowed for his troops. In vain was he told that, owing to the limited number of such arms available, he would lose his chance. He was adamant.

The tact, perhaps the personal intercession, of Lord Rawlinson, then the Commander-in-Chief, at length secured for the Maharaja his wish. Scindia won his "fight for the guns" and though he never lived long enough to see his batteries armed with 15-pounders or the addition of some pack artillery, he had the satisfaction of feeling that at all events the Gwalior State Forces would in future not suffer from the indignity of being utterly worthless so far as one of their most important arms was concerned. Victory had come at the end of his Thirty Years' War.

Never again would Scindia have the chagrin of seeing the moral effect of a carefully planned artillery exhibition wasted on those for whom it had been staged. The recollection of such a fiasco in 1923 had probably done much to stiffen his refusal to be deprived of the guns which he had expected, and indeed, if words meant anything, had been promised.

As a grand finale to his action against the Karera dacoits, of which a brief description has been given in the last chapter, he had decided to blow to pieces with his cannon the house of Baldeo Singh, perhaps the most notorious of the bandits who had surrendered. The house with a high watch-tower on its top was situate within a fortified village near Narwar. The fortifications were no towering ramparts, merely a thickish wall of mud and brick encircling the scarp on which the hamlet stood.

Baldeo Singh's house was a prominent mark on which to align the ordnance. The spectacle of the building crashing down, riddled by cannon balls, would demonstrate to the unruly of the district the might of the master who was determined that security and order should be the lot of the dwellers in all the territories through which his law ran.

The least ancient section of the State artillery was brought by its teams from the capital. According to the best traditions of manœuvre, fire was opened on the objective at a range of some seventeen hundred yards. From the first discharge of the ordnance it was seen that ranging shots were of little avail, as the guns would not carry anything like the requisite distance.

The villagers who had been made to vacate their houses to profit by the object lesson saw the cannon advanced bit by bit, first by fifty yards, then by increased distances, at last by a quarter of a mile until they were less than a hundred yards away from the fort wall. So far there had been a great expenditure of black powder and a considerable noise, but no apparent result. From close quarters the guns were trained on Baldeo Singh's house. At the given signal the whole battery fired at once. Forward, mostly along the ground, lollopped the cannon-balls. A few of those with the most force behind them even hit the base of the fort wall, maybe, though this is not established, dented its mud plastering, but anyhow rolled back much as do the balls trundled in an up-to-date skittle-alley with a return way.

That the bore of each piece was too worn to allow any cannon-ball to fit tightly rather than any defect in the locally made black powder was the cause which made accurate shooting an impossibility. As an object lesson in the power of artillery, the experiment had proved a dismal fiasco. In disgust the Maharaja ordered its abandonment. By its failure a part of his army had shown its ineffectiveness and His Highness was as jealous of his troops' reputation for capacity as he was of his own. This insistence on the need for efficiency comes out on every page of the volume of the "Darbar Policy" dealing with the Army Department.

That volume would hardly appeal to a pacifist. Uncompromisingly the Maharaja lays down such dicta as "it is the Army alone by means of which peace can be maintained," "it is a matter of primary importance to maintain an Army," or "it will not be out of place here to impress upon such people (those anxious to reduce military expenditure) the advantages which they themselves derive from the Army without which they could not find an opportunity to lead a life of ease and tranquillity and to devise means for their own welfare and prosperity, while comfortably lodged in luxuriously furnished houses. What a pity that they should think of destroying the very thing which affords them so much luxury and comfort!"

By its treaties with the British Government the Gwalior State is allowed to maintain a total force of all arms, regulars and irregulars, of between ten and fifteen thousand men. At the late Maharaja's accession the total strength was a little over twelve thousand and its cost about twenty-four lakhs annually.

Gradual reductions have brought the combatant strength of Scindia's Army to below seven thousand, though the cost has now risen to more than forty lakhs.

That the reduced forces of to-day are more effective than the larger army of three decades ago is admitted on all hands. The credit of bringing about the reduction in number and the increased efficiency must be given entirely to His Highness whose control over his troops was very real.

If in 1926 in their khaki uniform Scindia's Army be no such picturesque a sight as it was thirty years ago, at least it is at present able to render efficient aid to the British Empire in time of need. It can nowadays be mobilised for service outside the borders of Gwalior at the shortest notice. In it all the warlike castes to be found in the State receive equal treatment, and promotion is to-day the reward of work and capacity rather than of favour. For each of these results the prime credit is due to the soldierly instincts of Madhav Rao Scindia, to his innate dislike of any display which was not indicative of efficiency, to his equal regard for rank and file or officers apart from all religious or caste considerations, and above all to his wish to prove that his army was not meant for his personal glory but for loyal assistance to his allies, the British, in the hour of danger.

If he was no born soldier, natural aptitude and application made him no mean soldier, a fact to which a succession of Commanders-in-Chief from Lord Roberts to Sir William Birdwood have given genuine testimony.

It is largely due to his personal respect for discipline that to-day Scindia's Army shows as great a regard for that military virtue as the army of any Indian State. While expecting full value in the shape of work from his troops, he was ever solicitous for their comfort, and it was this solicitude, rather than any military genius, which attached all officers and men to him and aroused in them a genuine feeling of loyalty.

However able may be the conduct of the manœuvres during the next few years, the absence of Madhav Maharaj will be an irreparable loss, even if occasionally in the presence of some Commander-in-Chief or other distinguished general he might on a field day try to improve on the methods of attack as laid down in the Drill Book or by a series of dashing charges attempt the capture of the greater proportion of the artillery at the disposal of the force opposing him in mimic warfare!

He had far more of the soldierly spirit than the play spirit. Except at Canadian tennis he showed little aptitude for ball games. At lawn tennis he was a poor performer, at cricket a worse; for he had never been taught that game seriously. While he enjoyed playing games, he never looked on them as anything but pastimes. He held a deeply-rooted opinion that his country-men in most cases could not be great workers as well as great players. In his estimate they could never keep a due sense of proportion between their life's work and its amusements. He had a wholesome belief in games, especially in those which involved team-work, and in physical culture, but he always insisted that undue importance was attached to the play-side of life at all the Chiefs' Colleges, institutions which were a perpetual bugbear to him, although in two cases he retained his seat on their governing bodies. Their pupils, he contended, were taught to play but seldom to work, and as his opinions in committee never received due weight from the educational staff, the six-monthly meetings were only of use to him as an occasion to meet some of his brother chiefs and exchange with them views on other subjects than the upbringing of the young.

His build was not that of the ideal horseman, but nevertheless he was an exceptionally powerful rider with a good pair of hands. He was able to cover enormous distances in a day and yet be ready for work or *shikar* at the end of his ride. Motor cars, of which he had a great technical knowledge, used, he affirmed, to make him lazy, but, for all the motoring he did, once he was in the saddle, he seemed tireless. When on the box in charge of a team, he was an admirable whip, Colonel Crofts had seen to this.

During the impressionable years of his adolescence certain Indian Princes were polo-mad and spent a large proportion of the revenues of their States on the game. Despite his love of horse-flesh, Colonel Crofts with Sir

David Barr advised Scindia against devoting his energies to the game, and the inhibition, thus started, grew into a positive dislike for polo, though he would seldom openly admit the fact. He never encouraged its introduction among the officers of his Army and, even as a spectator of polo tournaments at Delhi or elsewhere, took but little interest in the players' skill.

At tent-pegging, the standard of which in Gwalior was very high, he was at least the equal of any and, year after year, would win the Gwalior Gymkhana Club Cup for that sport. But notwithstanding his excellence in such feats of horsemanship as usually figure in Gymkhana programmes, he was probably more interested in such competitions as Chart and Compass Races in which the rider had to use his brains as well as the speed and strength of his horse.

On both occasions, when visiting England, the Maharaja collected a scratch team from his suite or friends and easily beat Hurlingham in tent-pegging competitions, no mean feat considering that the horses used were all lent. During the competition in 1911 considerable excitement was caused as the horse ridden by His Highness suddenly took fright and bolted with its rider straight for a group of spectators. It seemed as if nothing could prevent a serious, perhaps a fatal, accident to the Maharaja or to some of the onlookers or to both.

Mad with fright, the horse tore along. Nothing could stop it. It was within a few yards of the stand which was crowded with onlookers. At the very last moment His Highness, who had bent forward and gripped the head-piece on one side, sprang off and slewed round the terrified animal which in an instant came to a surprised and shivering halt, facing away from the stand.

It was a great feat of equestrian skill and the only possible chance of averting a catastrophe. As a trick of Maratha horsemanship with a trained animal moving at a canter, it had been taught to His Highness in his youth, but with a strange mount that had completely lost its head and was tearing along full tilt it was a great piece of fortune that the result proved free from serious accident. The only comment that His Highness made was that it was a lucky fluke. It may have been so, but with any rider of less skill the fluke could hardly have happened. The newspapers made much of the feat, greatly to the Maharaja's disgust, and to end of his life it was always possible to raise his ire by a sly allusion to the title "Hero of Hurlingham" which one journalist had adopted as a catchy head-line in describing the occurrence.

With a shot-gun Scindia had been proficient from his youth and, though he neglected the art of bird shooting in his later years, he would usually top the bag at any impromptu duck shoot: but it was with a rifle and especially in a snap-shot at big game in the jungle that His Highness towered above the average *shikari*.

For its big game and especially its tigers Gwalior is famous. That the State Shikar Department is so admirably organised, is due in the main to the personal skill and innate jungle love which Scindia possessed. His own book on tiger shooting gives an admirable description of the peculiar methods that lead to success in that sport so far as Central India is concerned.

He was as capable as any of his *shikaris* in tracing the movements of a tiger and in luring it to its death. He expected no beater nor sportsman to undergo any danger which he was not ready, indeed anxious, to undergo himself.

In his tiger-shooting expeditions he had many narrow escapes. His *sang froid* on one occasion during the visit of the present King-Emperor to India as Prince of Wales saved the life of either Sir Stuart Beatson or Sir Pertab Singh, if not of both, when the Maharaja faced and dropped a charging tiger dead, literally at their feet.

He had many adventures with bolting elephants while following up wounded tigers and on such occasions, as always when in the jungle, his nerves were of steel, whatever might be the state of his physical health. His courage was of the highest and showed itself in the form of complete calmness in the presence of personal danger.

His close study of animal life and his almost instinctive knowledge of their ways frequently enabled him to set his *shikaris* right, when an expected tiger had failed to appear in the beat or had got away wounded or unscathed. It was organization alone, directed by his skill, that made possible such extraordinary results as the eight tigers in one beat, shot by Lord Hardinge and his staff, or the twenty-four tigers which Lord Minto bagged in three weeks: results which led to the erroneous theory (how it annoyed Scindia!) that the Gwalior tigers were fatted tigers and tamed to a high degree of domesticity.

How many tigers fell to Scindia's own rifle will never be known as he kept no count, but they must have been nearer one thousand than five hundred, if indeed their tale does not exceed the higher figure. Yet such a number did not imply indiscriminate massacre. The main breeding grounds, especially the wooded ravines along the banks of the Kuno River, were carefully left undisturbed, with the result that to-day there are probably more tigers in the Gwalior State than there were when His Highness received his ruling powers in 1894.

The shooting of tigers was strictly forbidden without the personal written permission of the Maharaja, since he regarded his tigers as a social and political asset to the State. Such rigorous preservation of big game entailed no hardship on his people, for in Gwalior man-eaters have been at all times rare. It gave him the greatest joy to receive informal visits from important personages and to let them enjoy the full advantage of his excellent *shikar* arrangements. On no occasion was Scindia a jealous shot himself, though he did not like the mild indiscretion of any Military Secretary or A. D. C., whose independent spirit might encourage him to take a snap-shot at a tiger as it was being driven up to a Viceroy's rifle.

The attractions of *shikar* in Gwalior brought to the State many notable persons of diverse nationalities with whom in the free life of the jungle His Highness became most intimate. It was possibly on such occasions that his fascinating personality made its quickest appeal to strangers, for he was a perfect and natural host who took a real delight in giving his guests the best of his sport and never made any attempt to intrude public matters into a private visit.

While intent on *shikar* or if watching, though not shooting, animals in the jungle, Scindia was absolutely unconscious of fatigue or privations of any kind, yet ever most solicitous of the personal comfort of any companion with him.

In former times Gwalior had been able to boast of lions as well as of tigers in its jungles. The last lion is said to have been shot near Goona in 1877. The gift of certain lion cubs from Lord Kitchener and the purchase of some more from Mombasa aroused in His Highness a wish to introduce lions once more into the State preserves.

The first attempt was a failure. Unused to life in the wild, the lions, freed from a comparatively small enclosure, were unable to fend for themselves and turned upon man as their easiest prey. Most of them were quickly recaptured and subsequently placed in a large enclosed portion of an uninhabited tract of wild jungle. From recent reports of lions shot on the borders of the State, as well as of one killed actually within the limits of Gwalior territory, there seems to be every prospect of the eventual success of the experiment, though the typical Central India jungle in no way resembles the usual lion grounds of Africa. Apart from questions of sport, sentimental reasons will lead the late Maharaja's many friends to wish that a scheme in which he took a deep interest may in the end come to full fruition.

In horse-racing, though he was at one time a moderately successful owner, moderately successful that is in consideration of the small size of his stable, His Highness only interested himself fitfully. He always maintained that when an owner had won a race and led in his horse amid cheers no credit was due to anyone except to the trainer and jockey, and certainly no credit attached to the man whose money had made him the owner. He professed to find but little pleasure in his own race-horses, since his many duties made it impossible for him to train and ride them personally.

He was fond of attending races provided his stay in Calcutta or Bombay coincided with some meeting, but he preferred the chance of seeing his friends or mixing with the crowd unnoticed and thus making new acquaintances to the racing itself. Considering his wealth, he betted very moderately and usually with ill success, though with very keen interest.

At his capital he constructed an excellent race-course at which meetings were held twice a year, but his object in the introduction of this sport was merely to attract people to the State so that they could see for themselves what material progress Gwalior was making, especially in his industrial schemes.

The spring and autumn meetings at Lashkar were pleasant interludes from hard work for the officials and people of Gwalior, but it is doubtful if the keen race-goers who came in only moderate numbers from British India ever seriously interested themselves in anything in the State beyond the race-course itself and the genial hospitality of their host. Though so long as the Maharaja lived the meetings were always kept up, they never paid expenses and have now wisely been abandoned.

There was never anything of the professional sportsman about Scindia, even in such lines as those in which he was an expert. His point of view was always that of the amateur who played the game for the game's sake, and who could take a beating well but would fight to the last to win, provided he could win by fair means.

While life is in them, he will never be forgotten by those who as guests or companions have had the privilege of joining in one of his tiger shoots. They know that not only was Scindia a charming host but that he was as well a sportsman, a genuine sportsman every inch of him.

CHAPTER X.

SCINDIA AS AN ADMINISTRATOR AND MAN OF AFFAIRS.

AS in the preceding pages may be found a brief account of some of the more prominent features of Scindia's life as a ruler, the necessity for any further reference to his activities as an administrator may be questioned. Such an addition, it may be urged, must in any case mar what little symmetry this memoir may possess. But any redundancy or lack of artistic arrangement will, it is trusted, be pardoned at least by those who had the privilege of intimacy with the late Maharaja. They are jealous that his memory pass not too soon into the night of ancient history and the limbo of forgetfulness through an imperfect delineation of his personality or an inadequate record of his achievements.

For this jealousy on the part of his friends there is good reason. Scindia, as a man, was far bigger than his work, though his work again was infinitely superior to his written or spoken defence of it. In his reviews on State Administration Reports or even in his *magnum opus*, "The Darbar Policy," as in his speeches, the late Ruler did himself scant justice. He had not the faintest appreciation of literary or rhetorical artifice. Even had he possessed such a gift, it is doubtful if his sense of pride would have allowed him to employ it. He was content, indeed he expected, to be judged by his actual deeds, and probably preferred those deeds to be criticised rather than left entirely unnoticed.

Born an autocrat, he lived and died an autocrat, and whatever may be the advantages of constitutional rule, none but a despot could in three decades have set Gwalior so far forward on the path of progress. At his accession his subjects as a whole had little or no understanding of or desire for anything but absolutism. They may not have believed in the theory of the Divine Right of Kings, but at least their Ruler held this belief, basing it on the consciousness, which with him was indeed no delusion, that the aim of all his public actions was the ultimate benefit of his people.

He refused to be daunted by the difficulties that faced him, by the lethargy of his subjects as a body, the active opposition to many of his earliest efforts at reform, and the mistrust of motives occasionally felt or expressed in high quarters. He never realised how severely handicapped he was by the lack of a thorough education, and this was fortunate, for, if he had weighed the theoretical advantages or disadvantages of each scheme he introduced before its introduction, he would not have left behind him so large a balance of success to his credit, even if his failures had been fewer.

To quote from an unsigned article in the issue of "The Jayaji Pratap" giving the tragic announcement of his death:—"To appreciate the labour, the energy, and the zeal expended by His Highness in triumphing over the difficulties that lay in his path we must throw our memories back over that amazing period from 1894 to 1910 when the foundations of the whole structure were laid. It is difficult to reproduce in these days of progress the atmosphere in which His Highness had to labour. It was an atmosphere surcharged with the apathetic belief that what is, is what ought to be. Intolerant of such a condition of affairs, His Highness set himself to the great task of reforming the administration. He had to cut his way through a tangled wood of vested interest, prejudice, tradition, and insularity—such as might well defy the genius of a whole generation of administrators.

"To understand him one must understand his conception of the office of a Ruler. According to him a Ruler is the servant of his people first, and Ruler afterwards. This is the whole gist of his doctrines. Some of these may be anti-academic, anti-scholastic, and anti-official but in their ultimate analysis all his doctrines, all his paradoxes, and all his teachings and practice will be found to conform to and converge on that one principle. Administration in his eyes was a matter of passionate vision rather than of logic, and there was in his estimation no system, no principle or rule of Statecraft so transcendent, so absolute, and so universal as could hold good for all time and all emergencies. He may be right or he may not, but certain it is that he was one of those practical mystics who at great historical conjunctures penetrate the deepest meaning of the present as it flies, and getting up all their being, thrust it forward on new and unknown paths. How things struck him, by what motives he was swayed, we never knew. And yet his decisions and conclusions were mostly right.

"His character was as various as his activities. On no shore did he burn his boats. His hand was in each department, the hand of a master. And when once he set himself to a task the latter seemed to possess every effective fibre of his being; the task and the man rolled into one. An impatient idealist, he was satisfied with nothing but the best. He expected to see in the work of men's feeble hands a full-length embodiment of the image of perfection which he had set up in his own mind. This feeling had gradually deepened into a ruling passion in him, and consequently faults and mistakes, no matter how trivial, often caused him inexpressible pain. His writings and utterances give one the impression of a soul in artistic distress rather than of a nature prone to finding faults. He was at times, it is true, too strong in condemnation of faults in others and was often led to fix on men words full of bitter irony and blistering contempt. But so magnanimous was his personality and so immeasurably greater was the man than what he said and did that all his condemnation, his censures, and his strictures would generally melt away in a moment without leaving the slightest scar on the memory."

His Highness regarded, indeed comported, himself as the servant of the State yet, it is doubtful whether in his heart of hearts he did not grudge the State having any other servant but himself! That he got through so much work as he did was due to the fact that, while he treated his officials as friends, he expected them all to slave as his personal servants and not as the servants of the State.

This conception, this assignment of *rôle* may, have been right or wrong. Judged by a certain standard of wise government, it may be said to have suited the conditions which Scindia found in Gwalior when he received his powers. It continued to make for discipline in the lower ranks of the services by imposing a direct check and making the subordinate officers' responsibility direct: but in the later years of his life, with the rapid growth of the ideals of responsibility and wise rule, it evoked some resistance and generated a conflict at least with some of those whom, in moments of clearer perspicacity, he did not hesitate publicly to designate as his colleagues and coadjutors. The habit of many years and its successful results prevented him from regarding with favour such resistance as begotten of a healthy sense of responsibility.

This result was inevitable. He had no wish to see arise in Gwalior a bureaucracy which, though making for the smooth and efficient public service he required, might yet act as a check on his initiative and so on rapidity of reform. To his view such an eventuality would be as bad as democracy, a system of government which had, he thought, frankly discredited itself in the eyes of all sensible people. Constitutionalism he regarded as a slow and cumbrous method, fraught with danger in most emergencies.

His unique personality made his officers accept with enthusiasm the part he gave them to play. Even if they thought he was wrong in some line of policy and had put their adverse view clearly before him, they still, under the spell of his compelling attraction, loyally did their utmost to bring to fruition even those measures of which they did not theoretically approve. It was thanks to such loyalty, a purely personal sentiment, that on occasions striking successes resulted where utter failure had been anticipated and predicted.

A word of explanation—if not indeed of credit—is here due to him and his officers. His administrative aims were always above cavil; his conceptions were original and, as such, often faultless. Thus all his schemes for the welfare of his people were fundamentally noble and bore the stamp of his imagination and resource: but, impatient idealist as he was, he wanted a short cut to the attainment of every end.

He was therefore never content merely to indicate a reform or suggest a line of amelioration. He must prescribe the method in every detail. It was here that the sense of proportion was often lost. Intense practicality ignored practicability; the pace set or the line of approach adopted often made the feasible impossible, and an incompatability developed between the aim and the method. There was sometimes so great a disparity between the object and the means that a complete divorce resulted, and projects that could have been worked or proved workable were, as practical problems, relegated to the sphere of idealism.

His officers did not desist from criticism and expostulation; often they attacked schemes with force and vigorously demonstrated their impracticability. But once he had overruled them, they loyally devoted themselves to the attainment of his aim. This peculiar loyalty was of a high order and a superior type, for, while applying his prescribed method, they often improved its detail with the single purpose of achieving the result desired.

They would all have confessed, or rather they all do confess, that for sane opportunism His Highness was always their superior. In an emergency none was so resourceful as he, none so ingenious, and none possessed of so practical a knowledge of the psychology of the people of Gwalior. When their master won a victory, for example in some big political case, they felt a genuine joy, and, if he had to admit defeat, they looked on it as a personal disaster. In the closing years of his life when, if his touch was as sure as ever, his grip on matters of State had begun to slip, they covered his mistakes with the greatest fidelity. Such devotion was no counterfeit. Scindia was loyally served, but it was personal loyalty. Compared with the man, his State seemed in his presence somewhat of an abstraction.

His service was hard and not too well paid. He had the peculiarity of expecting that any man who was fit for one position must be a success in any other office to which at a moment's notice, he might be translated, often against his deep personal inclinations. Again, while recognising the need of technically trained men in such branches of the State services as the Public Works or Forest Department, the Maharaja was always suspicious that the expert might not show enough "drive" as a departmental head, and so during the last few years of his life he adopted the system of non-technical "administrative officers" to control the ordinary routine work of their departments and to spur on the experts under them. That the system of administrative officers or the game of general post amongst departmental heads worked as well as it did is due at least as much to the horror of the officials concerned lest they should let their master down as to the sagacity displayed by that master in their selection.

Perhaps it was in his first judgments of individuals that His Highness showed less than his ordinary shrewdness. In picking a new man to fill a post, especially a stranger from outside the State, whether Indian or European, he often made serious mistakes, but he counterbalanced this weakness by the tenacity with which he clung to the services of any person of whose official work he approved. The voluntary retirement of such an officer he was apt to regard as an act of treason towards himself as their master.

Personal flattery did not cause Scindia much pleasure: but the flattery of his State and its administration always appealed to a soft spot in his nature. The State was his. He was master of it rather than Ruler of it, yet he regarded it as an heirloom more than as a piece of real property. To him Gwalior represented, as it were, a complicated piece of jewellery of which, owing to the neglect of its previous owners, parts had been lost or mislaid. Even if some of the lost fragments were gone beyond recovery, the mislaid parts might be found after careful search and replaced; but, in any case, all that remained must be polished up, made to look its best, and repaired when necessary. Some of the gems would look all the better for resetting, perhaps for rearranging; and some might even need recutting.

But all the polishing, resetting, and recutting must be done strictly in accordance with his own orders by the staff of craftsmen he had employed for the purpose. While he personally might make experiments, such daring on their part was taboo. Though he always deplored the lack of initiative in his servants, their sole duty was to obey orders and, woe betide them, if their work were not quick nor deft enough to satisfy their employer's notions. Because he was toiling harder than any of them, slack or slovenly craftsmanship was disloyalty to himself just as was any suggestion that the arrangement of the various parts as proposed by himself was not the best possible. It was, however, his foible to insist that the arrangement he adopted had been forced upon him by the failure of his unimaginative servants to suggest a better!

It was always a regret to him that all his craftsmen were not Gwalior-born. Local talent among his aristocracy must be trained and utilised as far as possible. His nobles held estates which had been given to their ancestors as rewards for services to the State, but that did not mean that the present-day holders should live lives of ease on the strength of achievements by their forebears. They must continue to work for the State.

Unlike his predecessors, Madhav Rao Scindia never bestowed on any of his subjects *jagirs* or hereditary money grants. While scrupulous in preserving ancient grants of land or cash allowances, he probably held that no service which anyone could render to the State was sufficient to justify a gift to a man's descendants in perpetuity. He might bestow a lump sum in cash as a reward to an individual, but he was not ready to mulct the State by a grant of an estate or money which would survive the man who had earned it by his services.

In taking this view he showed financial shrewdness. The richer the State was the more reforms and improvements it could carry out. For his own Privy Purse he fixed the amount he took from the Gwalior revenue at two per cent. In many an Indian State to this day no distinction is made between the private expenditure of the Ruler and that devoted to the general administration. Even in principalities where such a separation is made, the total taken for the Privy Purse usually ranges from five per cent of the total revenues upwards. No Prince to this day, it is believed, takes so small a portion of the total revenues of his State as did Scindia.

He made considerable investments in British India of the surplus balances left over from the public revenues, and these investments, from the time that the late Sir Shapurji Broacha was in charge, were, as a whole, most carefully chosen. But all these sums, principal and interest, were strictly earmarked as State money, not as his private property.

From these sums he created many funds to supplement the ordinary budgets of various departments. The interest could be used and even the principal, but the latter was solely reserved for productive works. Such action showed great wisdom, for, in a country where much of the revenue comes from the land and famines are frequent, it is necessary to have a substantial reserve.

None the less, while some of his financial measures ran counter to the accepted canons of Political Economy, he regarded adverse comment not only as rank financial heresy but as traitorous conduct. In his "Policy" he laid down that one-sixth at least of the total revenues must be saved each year. While such a procedure may be justifiable when an adequate reserve has to be built up, once such a reserve is already in existence it is hardly conducive to the general prosperity of a country that its people should each year pay out considerably more than is necessary for the normal expenses of government. Even if such excesses of income over expenditure be invested for the eventual good of the State, still those investments, being made outside Gwalior, do not immediately or directly help the subjects of the State, while, in no case, can the money circulate as quickly as it would do if it remained in the possession of individuals.

It is obvious moreover that the interest on funds available for reforms or extensions represents but a fraction of the amount that could be made available, were annual allotments not diverted to funds and thus locked up as capital.

This fact Scindia refused to recognise. Conscious that he intended the money for the good of the State as a whole, he was not prepared to discuss the general economic aspect of the matter. His object was to help his people who showed no great powers of self-help. As their master, he knew what was good for them better than they did themselves; as their servant, he would labour to achieve that good.

That in another matter the late Maharaja failed to appreciate the elements of Political Economy is illustrated by his views on indirect taxation. While he carried through reforms which resulted in an improved administration of his Excise and an increased income from that source, his policy as regards Customs is open to criticism.

The system of internal custom-houses, by which goods moving from one district of the State to another were mulcted for duties, he recognised to be gravely defective, and this pernicious arrangement he altered. Employees in the Customs Department who had not been regular State servants, now received the privilege of that service and became eligible for pension and gratuity, but the new arrangements made for the collection of customs duties included not merely tolls on goods brought into Gwalior but a levy on most of the agricultural products of the State when exported to British India.

Certainly the officials sitting at the receipt of custom became more honest than their predecessors, but the incidence of the export duties they collected lay undoubtedly on the original producers, that is to say, on those peasants whose interest the Maharaja had so much at heart. In buying their produce, the dealers—for the *ryots* do not export directly—naturally paid less than they would otherwise have done, since in their calculations of the cost at which they could put the goods on rail, they had to include the amount of the duties, and these were far from nominal.

In this case too Scindia was adamant. It was a question which he would not discuss on economic grounds. The increased revenue, drawn from these custom duties, was being spent or would be spent for the good of his subjects. He refused to admit that the ultimate effect of these export duties was the same as that of an increased rate of land revenue so far as the *ryots* were concerned. It must, however, in justice to him be admitted that, while adhering to this form of what he called indirect taxation, he did not mind how liberal were the land settlements made in the State or how great the remissions of revenue granted in famine years. He could see how such liberality directly benefited the cultivator; he could not visualise the harm done by heavy export duties, imposed on raw produce.

His greatest failures as an administrator were due to this limpet-like adherence to obsolete economic heresies. Were such false tenets attacked in the Economic Development Board by business men from British India, Scindia turned a deaf ear. This was his blind spot, where argument was a futile waste of time. The merchant prince who had criticised might be clever enough about his own particular business, but he had had no experience as the administrator of a State. Such people might even hold the preposterous idea that it was possible for a country which was raising loans to be prosperous! How could any State which owed money flourish? So dangerous a delusion must be censured in the "Policy."

Yet, if as an economist he was a failure, in other ways he was extraordinarily successful. His unorthodox views on Education, on the Legal Profession, and Justice, in no way hindered the advance of those three necessities of civilisation. Oppression of the poor, dishonesty, and disorder he put down with a strong hand. He gave his people security of life and property, speedy justice, improved communications, medical relief, and support in times of famine. No matter what might be the caste or creed of a man, provided he were a subject of Gwalior, Scindia treated him as if he were of his own religion or clan. He was absolutely free from any religious bias and would support a temple, a mosque, or a church with equal pleasure. Bigotry of any kind he abhorred and, though very particular himself about the performance of his own daily worship as a Hindu, he subscribed to the view of the Delphic oracle that the proper creed for a man was that to which he had been born. He was inclined to be suspicious of missionaries, not because of the doctrines they might wish to propagate, but since by experience he had often found them tactless and the unconscious agents of communal strife.

His success as an administrator lay not in his deep wisdom so much as in his personality. To quote from a shrewd critique of his qualities as a ruler, a sketch made in his life-time:—"He is in every sense a real ruler. All men in authority are apt to be assimilated by their surroundings and no constitutional governor is worth much after half a dozen years of office. The office spiders of the Secretariat are constantly at work upon such an individual and soon the cobweb of system closes in upon him. All constitutional governors—exceptions, of course, barred—are thus apt to fall an easy prey to little systems which have had their day and should have ceased to be. But the cast of His Highness's mind is different. Possessing within himself both resource and energy, he can, at any moment, wrest himself free from his surroundings and, when occasion requires, successfully rebel against the benumbing influence of all official and mechanical systems, break from their clutch, renew his contact with living forces, and cut new paths. His courage never fails him. It grows in intensity under the stimulus of unforeseen difficulties."

But it is not only as the Ruler of Gwalior that the late Maharaja Scindia deserves remembrance. In the wider field of public life in India he was—especially during his later years—a very prominent figure. He always held the view that while the Supreme Government could teach the Indian States a great deal, it could also learn much from them. It was from this belief rather than from vanity that he was of the firm opinion that the Indian Princes, either collectively or as individuals, should be frequently consulted on matters of common interest to British India and their States.

It is possible that His Highness valued the occasions on which his opinion was thus asked more than any of the honours bestowed on him by the Government of India. When, during the Viceroyalty of Lord Minto, he was first consulted on a matter of public importance, the actual problem being that of coping with the rise of sedition, his joy was a pleasure to watch. To his intimate friends he pointed out how wise was this new departure in policy. At last the Government was coming to his own point of view!

On such occasions he was tireless in giving his time and care to assist by his advice and, if necessary, by his presence, the Indian Government. As a whole, the advice he gave was sound and carried much weight among his brother Princes who time and again selected him as one of their spokesmen for urging upon the Supreme Government their special aspect of any matter. During the last decade of his life many Indian States, in determining what should be their attitude towards questions which concerned all the Princes and their territories, looked to Gwalior for their cue. If no diplomatist, but a believer in frontal rather than flank attacks, Scindia was always heard with attention, for he was wont to put all his cards on the table and to demand of the other side if their hand could beat his own.

His view never varied. His constantly expressed opinion was that the Government of India was the guardian of the rights and *izzat* (honour) of the Native States, and if the Government did not safeguard such *izzat*, the loss fell on it, not on the States.

He was not, however, merely a protagonist who fought on behalf of his brother Princes, he was too a most valuable ally to the authorities in cases where the welfare of India as a whole was concerned. A peculiar instinct enabled him to gauge the feeling that might be aroused by some administrative act on the part of Government. He pondered with great earnestness each matter on which his advice was asked, and the opinion which he gave was on all occasions fully considered and usually correct. Thanks to his acquaintance with persons in every grade of society and in every walk of life throughout the whole peninsula, he could generally present some new aspect of a matter which might have missed the attention of others. The language in which he would express his point of view might be faulty, but it was always forcible and revealed careful thought. With vivid illustrations and amusing anecdote he would preach the doctrine that "a country which is not governed on the basis of its own traditions can but go from bad to worse." While genuinely anxious for the growth of material and moral wealth in India, he did not think that this growth by any means postulated the introduction of democratic institutions.

During the Great War, at conferences, on committees, or in private lobbying, his natural ability and personality found a wide field for display. His services were invaluable and they were given most ungrudgingly. Throughout the unrest that in India followed the Armistice his unwavering support was of great use to a worried Government. In Gwalior, unlike many States, there was never the faintest suspicion of political trouble. Though he did not subscribe to the subaltern's point of view, "blow them from the guns, Sir," Scindia believed in a stern suppression of disorder, and his intimate knowledge of what was going on behind the scenes in the Swarajist camp was of much use in giving point to the opinions he offered on this subject.

Concerning the Montague-Chelmsford Scheme and the Reforms generally his opinions were somewhat inchoate. He saw the utility of the Chamber of Princes, but as regards the Assembly and the Council of State he subscribed to the view that, so far as the non-official element of members was concerned, those bodies would grow into "Kept Houses," representative of little but the important business interests of the larger cities. He had no hesitation in expressing his opinion that in British India, as elsewhere in the world, the times were out of joint, but he was also insistent that much of that dislocation was due to a lack of sympathy and understanding on the part of the official classes generally. By the "official classes" he meant both Europeans and his own countrymen, and would tell with gusto the story of how he was kept waiting for hours on the verandah of an Indian Member of the Viceroy's Council because the *chaprasi* to whom he merely gave the name "Scindia" would not announce his arrival without the receipt of a fee! He spent these hours of waiting in a discussion with the servants of the Member of Council on the great sense of dignity which had enfolded their master since his elevation to the proud position of Member of the Governor-General's Council for.........

One characteristic that distinguished the late Maharaja above many persons of greater intellectual attainments was his habit, when some public matter of which he had no intimate knowledge was under debate, of always remaining an attentive listener, and never speaking just for the sake of speaking. Instinct, as well as his innate tact, told him when to press a point with all the force of argument, when to withdraw so as to renew the discussion at some more favourable opportunity. In one volume of his "Policy" he gives naive instructions about the handling of men and officers, when to attack and when to retreat. He lays down a few simple rules as if they were the precepts of an abstruse philosophy and does not seem to recognise that it was his personality, rather than the dignity of his position or his astuteness, that secured him success in argument time and again. He had on occasion no fear in running counter to the general consensus of opinion, even to that of his brother Chiefs. Perhaps the most noticeable instance of this courageous trait was the attitude he adopted on the question of the Princes' Protection Bill to which a reference has already been made on a former page. At the same time he was also a zealous guardian of the rights of his fellow Princes and not merely a firm champion of his own.

While objecting strongly to the indiscriminate praise of any Chief who took little trouble with the administration of his State or the welfare of his subjects, he was at all times strongly opposed to the deposition of Indian Princes.

His views on this subject may with justification be stated at some length since, to judge from the report of a paper read and a discussion recently held at a meeting of the East India Association in March of this year (1926), his attitude in this question has been misunderstood.

In his review of one Administration Report for Gwalior occur the words: "Supposing that the Ruler or Rulers for the time being are not satisfactory individuals, the people should lead them on the right course by counsel."

This is a typical example of the way in which the late Maharaja frequently failed to do himself justice in his written words. By "the people" he did not mean a Ruler's subjects as was imagined by more than one Political Officer present at the meeting of the Association. Actually Scindia meant the people who are supposed to keep an eye on Indian Princes, and these were the Political Officers themselves! He held that the Government of India was inclined to give too much rope to a Chief who showed no sense of the responsibilities of his position, and thus the Rulers of Indian States were prone to lapse from bad to worse, when judicious advice, friendly admonition, or a clear statement of dissatisfaction on the part of the Supreme Government at an early stage might easily have corrected the fault before it became too late. Speeches, dripping with fulsome flattery, were delivered sometimes at State banquets or other formal occasions, when it was common knowledge among high officials of the Government of India that the individual praised was far from deserving laudation and when he himself knew it, and knew moreover that those officials were aware of it too. Such hypocrisy Scindia abhorred; apart from the ultimate evil effects on the Indian Prince, who was, in his opinion, actually encouraged to sink deeper and deeper into the mire of private vice and public misgovernment.

Should, however, a Ruler prove not amenable to advice and drastic action became imperative in the interests of his State in that event the view of the late Maharaja was that the wayward Prince should be summoned to appear before a committee of his fellow Princes where, by the judgment of his peers, it should be settled what action, short of deposition, should be taken in the matter.

The appointment of a judicial commission, as in the case of the ex-Maharaja of Nabha, was, he held, a gross mistake, besides being a confession that the Supreme Government must in the first instance have been remiss in doing their duty. By such an action they lowered their own *izzat* (honour) quite as much as that of the Prince whom they disgraced.

This attitude of Scindia may appear fantastic, but at least it was his honest opinion, and not the one with which he has been mistakenly credited. In spite of his words in the same review: "Wherefore, say no matter due to what reasons whether hereditary or congenital defects, evil counsel, or fondness for despotic power, if a ruler goes wrong, still keep him there in all his dignity," it is certain that the late Maharaja would have held one sin as unforgivable, one which justified the immediate deposition, perhaps the actual execution, of the offender. Only one crime merited such treatment, and this was the crime of active treason to the British Crown, a sin which he held unthinkable for any Indian Prince.

At all events he was on firm ground in remarking that "repeated depositions and interregnums are shown by history to be occasions for intrigue," his remark made in the same context. It is a fact that the enforced abdication or removal of an Indian Chief is looked upon by his subjects as a personal calamity and an unmerited disgrace to themselves even by those who in actual fact may have suffered terribly from his misrule. Without any appeal to history or perhaps to reason, they agree with the views of the late Maharaja. Instinctively they feel that there is something unnatural for a son to be ruling while his father is still alive, or, if he be a minor, they give no credit to any regency administration, however able; for they miss the personal touch of a despot, whether good or bad, just as they miss the fascinating occupation of discussing the foibles of their Prince and their possible effect on themselves.

It is strange that the part which Madhav Rao Scindia played on the stage of British India in the last decade of his life attracted little notice or interest among the people of Gwalior as a whole. This may have been due in part to the fact that he always had his name and his doings kept out of the Press as far as possible. He would sneer at the vanity which led some petty chieftain to announce in the papers that a tiger had fallen to his rifle or informed the world that some unimportant Maharaja had introduced a trifling reform with which his subjects were represented to be overjoyed. Whether he worked or played, Scindia eschewed publicity and in British India or in Gwalior liked to pass unnoticed.

Whatever the reason, his subjects scarcely recognised that he utilised his visits to Delhi or Simla, Calcutta or Bombay to deliver shrewd blows in secret against those whom he held to be subverting the political structure of India. His people would have preferred to have had their "Madho Maharaj" constantly among them and ordering them about, even if their compliance with his commands might not be so exact nor so prompt as he wished.

Yet, at however low an estimate we assess the work of Scindia outside his own State, at least that work brought him many a time respect instead of suspicion, and open friendship in place of veiled hostility. In the *Gazette of India Extraordinary* referring to his death there may be read between the lines a genuine grief at the passing of one who on a wider platform than Gwalior had usually played a big part well and oftentimes with distinction. In official matters he had often helped, and had often fought with, the Supreme Government, but on all occasions his help had been disinterested and his methods of fighting indisputably fair.

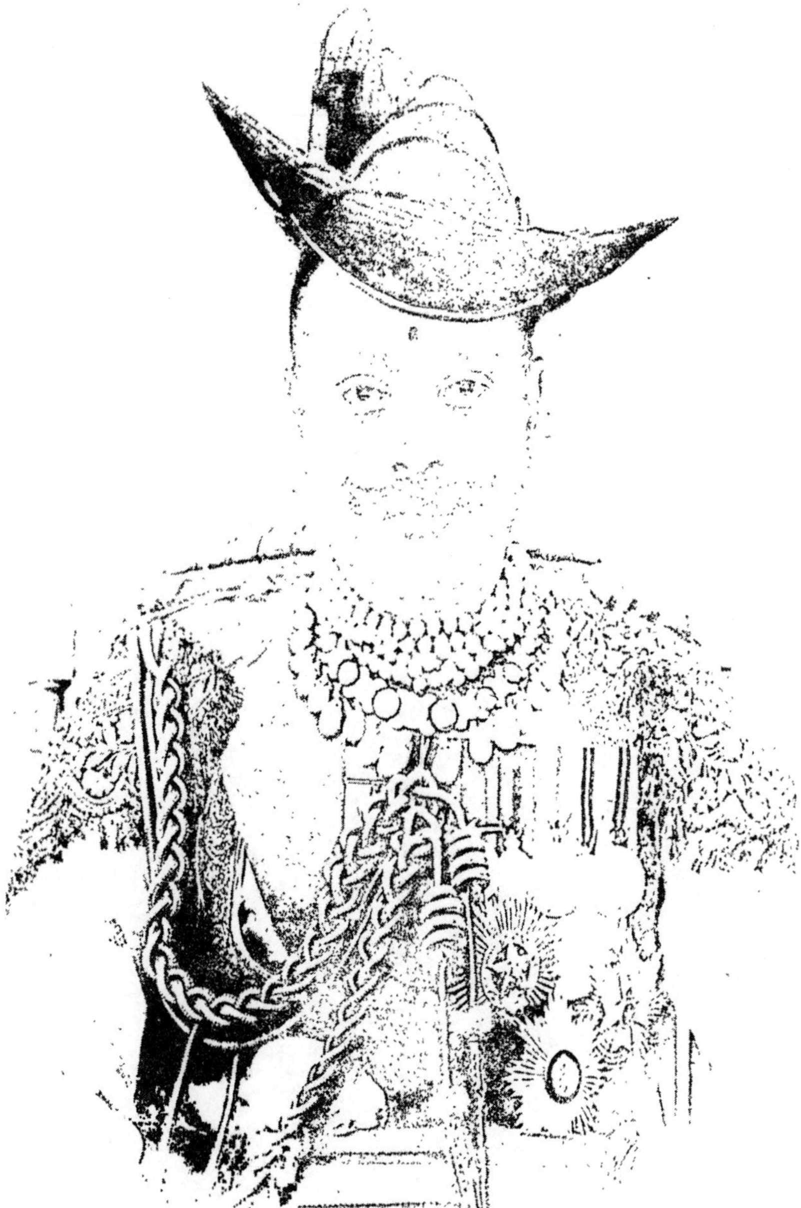

CHAPTER XI.

SCINDIA, THE MAN.

"MINISTERS of good things," Hooker has said, "are like torches, a light to others, waste and destruction to themselves." The simile is apt for "men of great and noble obsessions," the arresting generalisation exemplified in the personality of Madhav Rao Scindia. To his subjects and to his friends he was undoubtedly "a minister of good things," both spiritual and material. If among his equals he contented himself with being merely "a light to guide," for his servants and dependants, when necessary, he without effort became "a rod to check the erring and reprove." To himself he was "waste and destruction." Perversely he threw away his life: yet the tragedy of his premature death is in part lightened by the reflection that the earnest, almost the enthusiastic, process of waste and destruction sprang from a conscious and deliberate effort to minister to the good of his fellow-men.

An anonymous, but penetrating, estimate of Scindia published within a few months of his death gives a graphic picture of the man:—"Physically a mere shadow of his former self, he is yet the liveliest and most vibrant of men. Indeed it is a question whether his quick responsiveness does not sometimes assume the form of a hyper-sensitive reaction to the feeblest impulse. At all events, the peculiar characteristic of his more than human energy seems to be a love of the formidable. And his method of overcoming obstacles is not the flanking, but the frontal, attack. One might say he had a passion for proving possible the apparently impossible. This disposition alone must wear him out: at any rate, the satisfaction derived from indulgence in such physical Quixotism is beyond the mere normal man's power to gauge.........

"Hearty, earnest, tenacious, quick of grasp, but quicker of temper, holding fast to his convictions, but faster to his friends, suffering hardships gladly, but fools less gladly, alternately relentless and flowing with emotion, such as he is, he is a most magnetic personality, difficult to resist, still more difficult to shake off."

To be thoroughly frank about the late Maharaja of Gwalior can take away nothing from the honour justly due to his memory. All his failings were due to a lack of elasticity in his moral temperament. Angular, enigmatic, intangible, he had his own way of judging conducts and determining his course of action. His prejudices were strong and often his very acuteness led him to the verge of excess. He had a stubborn faith in his own perspicacity which made him impatient with difference of opinion. This, a mere tendency in youth, in middle age set into a habit and was mainly responsible for the over-emphasis and ill-balance of many of his latter public acts and utterances.

He became more and more intolerant of small blemishes, and his wrath found expression in language which justly gave offence even to those most devoted to him.

Apart from the twelve volumes of "Policies" which he wrote and published, the series of thirty-six "Memoranda," which he has left, all resulted from this intolerance of the imperfections natural in his chosen instruments of administration.

While the "Policies" themselves are a store of patient work and important thought, no biographer could give so clear a picture of Scindia in every aspect of his innermost self as he has given himself on many a page of this in one sense monumental achievement. These volumes at once reveal the breadth and narrowness of his mind and bring out all the strong contrasts in his temperament. The boldness of their language is singularly typical of the man. In this work, which he intended to leave the world as his swan-song of justification, he lets himself go absolutely in his attempt to divide his likes from his dislikes, to formulate his doctrines, and to enforce his preferences and dogmas, with a pertinacity that is pathetic. The attempted search after Truth degenerates into a violent effort to drag Truth to his side, and the most uniform feature of this uneven work is its pedantic rectitude. Of the dozen or so volumes that on the administration of Justice, in which he declares war on universally accepted principles, is perhaps the section most characteristic of him.

But the "Policies" were the last effort of Scindia's failing years, and his memory must be protected against the harm that his book may do it. Such is the reason, if not the justification, for this chapter which, apart from being inartistic, must in the nature of things prove formless and inchoate. No theory will be advanced about the composite personality of the late Maharaja, but in its delineation justice and sincerity will be kept in view. An attempt will be made to exhibit his temperament to the public gaze in the hope that through the representation, however inadequate, a glimpse will be got of Madhav Rao Scindia as a man.

Perhaps Francis Grierson is right in insisting that "character distinguishes one man from another and gives identity; true personality distinguishes one man from all others, and gives originality. Every human being that lives a sober industrious life possesses character, but neither sobriety nor industry will give personality. The quality of character is limited to local environment, the quality of personality is universal in its influence, and originality is its fundamental element."

In a dispassionate analysis Madhav Rao Scindia shows himself possessed of even more personality than character, and, above all, of a singular originality.

Pope Pius IX is credited with the remark that the circle of every man's acquaintanceship is divisible into four quadrants. We like and understand a person or we like but misunderstand him; we dislike and understand him, or we dislike but misunderstand him. Of the late Maharaja it may be affirmed, however, that while for every one man who understood him there were ten that did not, for every one man who did not like him, there were twenty that did. Further, while all who really understood him liked him, even many of those who did not, liked him all the same and just as much. He had the personal magnetism which compelled affection not only in those whom his varied conduct puzzled but even in such as thought him hard, calculating, and relentless.

In the matter of mere physical qualities he had few advantages over his fellow-men. In height he could not top five-foot-six, though, to make the most of his inches, he held himself very erect. Until wasted by disease in his later years, his figure was stout and rounded, but this incipient corpulence did not affect the strenuous activity suggested by his upright and alert, if somewhat stocky, frame. Distinctly broad-shouldered, he had too a development of calf that was striking. His face was saved from the commonplace by his eyes, an inheritance from his mother. They were large, and prominent, yet withal piercing, and apt to detain the casual glance of passers-by. There was an attraction in their dark-brown depths, whether at the moment they expressed joy or sorrow, real or mock gravity, pensive thought or humour, candour or mystery. In them his friends usually found a clear index of the underlying mood; no infallible index, however, for, when roused to anger, His late Highness, if he thought a display of temper impolitic could keep the expression of his eyes as serene as that of his mouth, his father's mouth: but on such occasions he could not control the twitching of his fingers and, to conceal this danger signal, would often clasp his hands behind his back.

When in uniform or in the splendour of Darbar dress, the Maharaja would turn himself out right regally; yet he cared nothing for personal adornment. He liked comfort in his clothes; but their age, cut, or general appearance concerned him not in the least. He found an active pleasure in passing unrecognised by those who would have done him honour, thanks to the unintentional disguise of an ill-fitting pair of *khaki* slacks with a patched and ancient *shikar* coat on top.

He loved seeing humanity in all conditions and from all aspects and loved even more being mixed up in a harum-scarum crowd, a trifle flustered and agitated,

During every railway journey, after night-fall, he, in the scantiest of apparel, would leave his saloon at each stop of the train, to be jostled by the crowd on the platform. On such occasions he was not playing the ferret; rather he wore the look of abstraction, as if he were keener to drink in experience than to observe or to descry. It was exactly this attitude of mind that alike sent him searching the seamy side of life in Europe and, during his tours in his own State, led him to the door of some poor peasant to share with him a meal of *juar* bread and butter-milk.

With his innate abomination of all finery, he seldom wore any of his wonderful jewels, though once, as a boy, when taking the part of a king in a play he had written, he carried heroically on his person a weight of over fifty pounds of pearls, emeralds, and diamonds! This dislike of ostentation was no more a pose than was his complete disregard of physical comfort in such matters as food or the appointments of his palaces.

When Madhav Rao Scindia was but seven, his father had shrewdly prophesied: "He will not be as lavish with gifts as Maharajas usually are. He will enjoy but little ease and comfort and will constantly move about. Of the good things of this world he will appropriate but a small share. He will eat ordinary food and wear ordinary clothes, but he will earn a great reputation for himself."

In a well-worn suit and unattended, Scindia liked to pass incognito, maybe to visit some shop where he was quite unknown and make his private purchases, or perhaps to test the vigilance and discipline of his guards. Outside his State, his simple garb was often a calculated device to expose the pretensions of the underling on duty who respects appearances more than the essential principle of his responsibility.

When buying anything, he delighted in driving a bargain, for he refused to believe in such things as fixed prices. To him the nickname of "*Bania Maharaj*" was a matter of pride rather than of resentment: but it is questionable if he deserved congratulations on his efforts to act the part of a private gentleman of moderate means in preference to that of a wealthy potentate who scorned to haggle. In India at least the astute vendor knew him and, in quoting a price for his wares, invariably allowed for a drastic cut. In such intelligent calculations the Arab horse-dealer of Bombay was an easy first in the race for Scindia's opulent stakes and always got the better of his customer. The remarkable private bargains struck between both parties always ended in the complete satisfaction of the buyer and the lucrative victory of the seller. Never did any other transactions provoke in the disinterested spectators a wider range of mixed feelings, pity and resentment, amusement and indignation.

Yet, while Scindia would not pay a penny beyond his notion of the proper price for anything, he was always most scrupulous about the immediate settlement of his debts. This was a point of honour with him, and on honourable conduct in this respect, as in others, he held strangely rigid views that may indeed be regarded as typical of his baffling personality. No suzerain could be more generous and indulgent to his feudatories than was Scindia to his Sardars. The improvident noble and impecunious landowner would often apply to him for a loan and never apply in vain. Similarly, to set an encumbered estate on its feet, he, unasked, would substantially reduce for a term of years or forgo entirely the tribute due by it to the State: but, if any condition on which he granted such accommodation were not fulfilled or an instalment to be paid were withheld, no matter in what circumstances, it is correct to say that in every such case—probably from what may be called a principled indignation—his mental equilibrium was completely upset. So strong was he on this article of his personal code that he did not hesitate to apply it even to social institutions. As president of the leading club in Gwalior on more than one occasion, by an easy confusion of *rôles*, he ordered the Finance Department to settle the club account of some member in arrears by a deduction from his official salary. In a social matter such an autocratic act was typical of the man.

When travelling, he kept his receipts and private accounts most carefully; and it would worry him greatly if he failed to recollect the exact details of any expenditure, however small.

So long as his health remained fairly good, he was careless of variations in climate or temperature. Taking advantage of the long days, he would do his hardest work during the hottest months of summer and do it in conditions which made his officers gasp for breath. Oddly enough he disliked a fan in his office and would throw all the doors and windows open to let in the scorching "*loo*" and, to ward off the drowsiness which is inseparable from its heat, he used snuff freely to keep his brain clear.

Throughout his life punctuality in the hours for his meals was foreign to his nature, though he was inclined to criticise any such irregularity in others.

In sickness and especially when suffering acute pain, he was a man of great fortitude who was the despair of his doctors and a marvel to all around him. Many can recall occasions when never a moan escaped him though, while suffering from dyspnœa, his eyes looked as if they would shoot out of their sockets or he writhed in agony from cramps in his legs. He hated whining and made as light of the sufferings of others as of his own, thus often giving the impression of callousness: but in reality none felt more deeply for true affliction than he, and nobody knew better how to revive drooping spirits or to rally the despondent. His humanity was broad, and with mourners he was tenderness itself. His inexhaustible energy enabled him to manifest his sympathy in a very practical form. To his officers on their death-beds he was the embodiment of generosity, unremitting care, devoted compassion, and an inspiriting exaltation.

He was a man of deep faith and, whatever opinion may be held of its nature, that faith inspired his conduct. He believed in Divine intervention, indeed he was convinced that Providence was amenable to prayer and that charity averted misfortune. This may be scoffed at as "simple faith," but his tenacious hold on it endowed him with great firmness of decision and with courage that never quailed. Justice he believed to be invulnerable with the result that he studied the ethical side of things and, when he believed himself to be in the right, his conduct was always unflinching. The effect of his occasional disillusionments was pathetic, and, in some junctures, he touched bathos. At the same time every calamity left him with a fund of practical resource and in a thoroughly philosophic mood.

Though there were really few folds in his temperament, perhaps no secret places in his heart, it is not easy to bring into relief his actual personality. No one knew better than he how to keep apart official and private relations: in the latter he combined the sweetest indulgence with inexorable sternness in the former. The combination puzzled many people, but it may, perhaps, be regarded as the strongest ingredient in his character as well as the best proof of its balance. The closest intercourse with his officers he loved, as also to be entertained by them without extravagance and strictly according to their means. When thus a guest, he was a friend amongst friends, and there was no air of condescension about him. He felt hurt when denied the opportunity of such intimate association; such denial indeed he interpreted as expressing personal disapproval. So genuine was his sincere desire to be identified with his friends that he welcomed the request for advice in their private and domestic concerns and freely reciprocated such confidences. He appreciated as a compliment his appointment as executor in the wills of some of his officers. The responsibilities of such a position he discharged with meticulous care at great sacrifice to his leisure and always to the benefit of his wards.

Nevertheless, no matter how close his relations with his officers, neglect of duty found in Madhav Rao Scindia an implacable censor. As synonymous therewith he treated apathy and irresponsibility. This trait was exemplified by his treatment of his *Jagirdars* and other grandees all of whom he expected to do their best for the State. He refused to let Gwalior be the paradise of the rich and the purgatory of the poor and demanded that property should pay ransom for the security it enjoys. While he held hereditary rights sacred, he insisted that the rights of the State were entitled to an especial reverence, a reverence that should take the form of service. When accused of sternness in his treatment of any noble who showed no aptitude for hard work, he would retort in his direct manner "I don't slack and I don't mean to let anyone else do so." However highly placed the culprit might be, when judging laziness or indeed any delinquency, Scindia maintained a heart of stone. Corruption he never forgave; but visited it with condign punishment.

He was no great reader of books; indeed it would be correct to say that he was "without a tincture of literature." Such intellectual interests as he had were in the domain, or rather on the outskirts of the domain, of Military History and Science. At night, if he could not sleep, he might occasionally run through a detective story and now and again would claim to have gained ideas of practical worth from some such book; but on the whole he was fonder of "The Scientific American," a periodical which he studied with deep interest until one day he ordered a motor plough, depicted in its pages as at work, only to find that the plough had not been actually manufactured, but only advertised. After that day he never opened the magazine again, but gave the American Consul in Bombay his views on the whole subject of the phantom plough and the immorality of such extravagances of publicity.

For the ornate and the picturesque in style he had no admiration; in fact he always regarded the rounded period with distrust and as an attempt "to throw dust in people's eye" or "to pull their legs," to quote two of his "idioms." And yet, though no phrase was for him arresting, some words by their sound annexed his fancy. One such word was "criterion," "insomnia" was another; and both of them he strangely distorted when he used them himself.

For music Scindia had a genuine appreciation and, in a voice that was somewhat thin and shrill, sang with great expression and in perfect tune. Otherwise he had no æsthetic tastes. In painting, architecture, *belles lettres*, and the fine arts generally he had little interest, though his fondness for beautiful scenery was real and unaffected. While repairing some fine old building, he would often replace a magnificent fretted stone verandah by a crude erection of corrugated iron and fail to notice, or perhaps deliberately would ignore, the resulting incongruity. "I must have my little joke" he remarked with a malicious chuckle, when an architect had left his presence almost in tears on being ordered to perpetrate an atrocity of this nature. He knew that, despite protestations, the architect in this case would sell his art for mammon.

Throughout his life he retained his interest in machinery and would spend hours tinkering at any unsatisfactory car in his garage. More than once he stripped a Rolls Royce of its engine and fitted it in a cranky boat which he had bought as a bargain secondhand. Next to the administration of his State, nothing, perhaps, gave him in his later years so much pleasure as an exploring trip in a motor launch, whether on the river Chambal or on the Tigra or Chandpatha lakes, or again in the creeks near Bombay. Water held no terrors for him. A good sailor and an excellent swimmer, he would enjoy seeing how far he could go without running his launch on a sand-bank or rock. He was fond too of touring in a barge on which he could have his meals and sleep out, if necessary.

Outings of such a kind were a delight to him, for they usually included the cooking of food in the jungle. By universal consent a competent *chef,* he always found far greater satisfaction in the preparation of his meal than in the subsequent eating of it. Towards the close of his life, these expeditions probably amused him more than the serious work of *shikar.* His love of being on the water grew with his years and led to the construction of such engineering feats as the Bhagora canal or the upper and lower lakes at Chandpatha. For complete happiness he would spend hours wading while towing and shifting house-boats or possibly toiling to refloat some launch which he had run aground on a previous trip.

In all such amusements he expected his officials to take an active part; indeed, in some ways, he can hardly be said to have had a private life at all, for he was seldom happy unless he had a number of his officers and friends about him. So much did he favour constant associations of this sort that, even in trying illnesses, when other men would have chosen to be left alone, he demanded to be surrounded by a rollicking company. He abhorred the long face at any time; always it provoked him to mordant sarcasm.

All his waking moments he wished to be shared by cheerful temperaments the continual presence of which afforded constant scope for the practical jokes of which he never tired. The first of April at times became almost an official, if a non-gazetted, holiday and on that date, or indeed on any other, should a practical joke turn against himself, Scindia was at least as amused as anyone.

On a pleasure outing the only distinction that he made between himself and his guests was that he, if he liked, might talk "Shop," but woe betide any of them, if they did. The want of heart-felt interest, nay enthusiasm in the pleasure scheme of the moment, invariably aroused his feelings, and he seldom forgave manifestations of boredom if resulting from the peculiar enjoyments that he had been at pains to provide.

He could relax in a wonderful fashion; yet at the back of his mind the whole time was his State and its welfare. So much was this a fact that it might be urged that his outlook was parochial, for, wherever his body moved, his mind dwelt in the narrow microcosm of Gwalior which he apotheosised. But a juster estimate would be to recognise that his absorption in his State only gave the measure of his sense of duty. Whatsoever might be the sport on hand, he was always watching his companions and trying to sum up their weak and strong points. If on a cooking picnic an officer feigned a pleasure which he did not feel, Scindia could detect the pretence in a moment; for, whether at work or play, his shrewd vision let little escape it, and his policy at all times was to make use of any person according to his estimate of the other's capacity. whether he liked him or not. The use thus made was seldom for his private ends; generally it was intended for the ultimate benefit of his State. Some of his greatest failures sprang from the employment of some individual whom he did not trust but whose ability (as he visualised it) he could not bear to leave untried.

In his judgments of capacity as well as of character he often made mistakes despite his assiduous watchfulness. He was no more a natural judge of a man than he was of a horse.

Beaconsfield has said:—"It is better to be impudent than servile." So the remark may be hazarded that Madhav Rao Scindia's mind was a strange compound of insight and obtuseness, of genius and ineptitude. At intervals he saw things which others did not see; often he was inconceivably blind to much which almost everyone saw. He had too a marvellous faculty of self-deception and a morbid streak which in time affected both brain and will. Such morbidity in his later years he often expressed in words which meant

"Let me not live...........
After my flame lacks oil, to be the snuff
Of younger spirits."

It is because of his wonderful admixture of contradictory qualities that Gwalior, which without him is ridiculous, was, at times, with him impossible.

Yet, despite a few blemishes, of good qualities how full a measure had he! He had vision, courage, and ambition, all joined to a strong sense of duty. He pictured to himself the future and laid his plans to win accordingly. The ferment in India during the last few years of his life led him to realise that the best security for his position lay in deepening the personal attachment of his people to him, an attachment which was ever great. He appealed to the imagination of his agriculturists and, as part of his tacties, in public utterances spoke of his *zamindars* as his "*annadatas*" (bread givers). To his credit be it said that his tactics were not evanescent. He was not content merely to flatter the vanity of his *ryots*: unflaggingly he worked for their welfare.

He had a genuine and outspoken hatred of the arid plain of democracy where "every mole-hill is a mountain and every thistle a forest tree." He regarded all demagogues as the commonplace of history and held that they were to be found wherever popular commotion had prevailed and that they all bore a strong family likeness one to another. Such men he did not fear, but challenged and defied. In politics, as in other matters, he had no belief in the premonitory shadows of coming events: on the contrary, he maintained that "upheavals give no timely warning; one must always be prepared for them."

A master of detail, he showed great powers of anticipation when creating an organization for a big public occasion: but he lacked method. He was by nature very accessible and always condemned those who by habit were not so, since he held that "the Ruler and the ruled should meet as often as possible, if there is to be identity of aim and interest between them." This, like many of his remarks, may be a truism, but he was at least man enough to live up to his platitudes. For example, he acted in strict accordance with many of his commonplace sayings such as:—

"People with assured incomes can afford to be idle, those without can't. I am one of the latter class."

"Be slow to decide, but never slow to act."

"To find fault is easy, to avoid fault hard enough."

"I want the consciousness, not the credit, of accomplishing a job."

"Testimonials and certificates are snares."

His private ambitions ranged from making his administration a model of efficiency to excelling personally in the art of healing. He lanced abscesses as often as the sufferers would let him and for long, as a boy, strove to induce an I. M. S. doctor, the brother of his "Guruji," to teach him "Eye Operation."

His ambitions never led to log-rolling, and in the matter of decorations he did not importune the authorities to multiply the stars upon his breast. Decorations might flatter the owner's personal vanity, but they did not increase the dignity of a State; so he would contend. Still, if a secret may now be revealed, he vainly coveted the Knighthood of the Garter ("there's no damned merit about it") as a counterblast to the exaltation of Highnessship. Such a unique honour to its Ruler might, he thought, enhance the reputation of Gwalior in the world at large.

He had no need of decorations to attract attention, for his circle of acquaintances in India was enormous and comprised persons in every grade of society. For instance, he seemed to know from individual contact every stationmaster on the line from Delhi to Bombay, just as he knew all the prominent business men of the provincial capitals or the leaders of every section of Indian thought and politics. He was an admirable host, and the hospitality which he extended with true pleasure was as lavish as it was free from all vain display.

His Christmas camps, held at Gwalior for many years, grew to be most popular functions, invitations to which were eagerly sought. Two fancy-dress dances, at which His late Highness would appear in some remarkable costume of his own invention, were always a prominent feature at these camps. Never dancing himself except in the frolic of Sir Roger de Coverley, he was very fond of the informality which fancy-dress lends to any entertainment; and on such occasions he was always at his merriest whether, in the garb of a "Microbe," he was hanging on to a doctor's coat-tails or was sprawling at an old lady's feet and begging her to sit on him, in his disguise as an Egg, to prevent his growing addled!

During his waking hours—and he seldom slept for more than four hours at night—Scindia was rarely to be seen without a cigarette in his mouth. This he in later years varied with a pipe, but he never stuck to any one brand of cigarettes or smoking mixtures for long. He attempted no brain work without tobacco, which indeed played a more important part in his adult life than did food. If he ever sat meditating over an office file and was not smoking, the probability was that in that file he had discovered something most annoying to him. His last request was for a cigarette.

In private life, as in public, he found devoted service and was indeed a hero to his valet, but he would never admit that he was well served, for he had a curious idea that such an admission might be subversive of discipline. His personal attendants he treated with especial kindness, yet, except for an occasional nod of approval, he never praised them for the careful assiduity of their ministrations.

It was, perhaps, his physical courage which made a deeper impression on his retinue than any other of his virtues. By experience they all knew that he was afraid of no living creature except the diminutive house-lizard which for some inexplicable reason aroused in him an unconquerable horror. This innocuous reptile, the smaller it was so much the more was it terrifying, could rout the man who never turned a hair when, as happened on several occasions, he had to stand his ground and face a charging tiger.

In the display of moral courage too, Scindia was an equally queer admixture. He would himself, if occasion demanded, run counter to custom or to caste prejudice, and, in such a case, would expect his companions to do the same. Yet he was inclined to look askance on independence of thought or action in similar matters, if displayed by his subjects, and especially so, if such independence exceeded the limits he had set for himself. For example, the custom of the *purdah* he converted into a mere form instead of retaining it as a rigid obstacle to social intercourse; but he did not approve of its entire abandonment, perhaps because he very definitely held that the activities of Woman should be confined to domestic affairs alone. Any part she played in public life should be no open one. Enough for her to be mistress of the house with her interests centred on her children, the kitchen, and a true companionship to her lord and master, whensoever he demanded it. In matters of social reform generally he was amusingly inconsistent, orthodox and iconoclast both claiming him as their own and seldom without good reason.

He was very fond of children and quickly gained their affection, not merely because he would always make time to play with them, but more, perhaps, because he ever treated their ideas with serious gravity and could enter into their views of life in a way that comes naturally to few "grown-ups." In some ways he possessed the spirit of "the boy who never grew up," and his jokes, particularly those he perpetrated on his mother or on persons of whom he was especially fond, were often horribly annoying. Whether any of his jests came off or failed, indeed if anything amused him, he would give vent to a happy chuckle for which he was well known throughout the length and breadth of India and which by its infectious nature on many occasions led him to make new friends when among strangers.

Madhav Rao Scindia was not only a devoted son to his mother: he always realised too that he had occasion to be a grateful one. To him her death was a shock which brought in its wake a disillusionment quite unwarranted and entirely peculiar to his fond, masterful, and rather self-deluding nature, a disillusionment, moreover, which the collapse of his health and nerve visibly hastened. He grew more and more superstitious and after her demise would, while at Shivpuri, spend most of his so-called leisure hours in or near her mausoleum. Within that shrine he would intently watch her face, so admirably reproduced by a Bombay sculptor. When thus occupied, he oftentimes sought solutions of the dilemmas in which he found himself and held the belief that he knew her mental, and indeed her physical, state in the ethereal regions above from the passing expressions his fancy pictured on her face. In this matter he became increasingly credulous, until, remarking the fact, the attendants at the cenotaph, so as to curry favour, affected personal conviction and retailed what a sceptical age can but regard as pure inventions. For example, one hot summer's day in Shivpuri the Maharaja worked himself into a rage at the negligence of his electrical staff. The fans had stopped, and he had been told that in consequence beads of perspiration had been seen standing on the forehead of his mother's statue !

Without venturing an opinion on the visibility of disembodied spirits, it may be said that the stories current as to the reappearance of His late Highness in ghostly form ring true to sentiment. On at least two occasions after his death, his figure is reported to have been seen entering or leaving the mausoleum of "Jija Maharaj." It is fitting that his own *chhatri* of white marble is now being raised near to hers in accordance with the wishes expressed in his will.

Yet, however superstitious Madhav Rao Scindia became towards the close of his life, he never lost the pluck of Montaigne's mariner who in a great tempest said to Neptune "O God, thou mayest save me, if thou wilt; and, if thou wilt, thou mayest destroy me; but whether or no I will steer my rudder true."

Had he studied philosophy, it is likely that Scindia would have preferred the maxmis of Montaigne to those of far profounder thinkers. For instance, in matters of religion the late Maharaja held that "nothing is so firmly believed as what we least know" and that "everyone's true worship is that he finds in use in the place where he chances to be;" in politics that "it is so much to be a king that he is only so by being so:" as regards Fate, that "our wisdom itself and the wisest consultations for the most part commit themselves to the conduct of chance:" and in private life that "a little play is desirable in those that will not be guilty of stupidity."

While believing that so far as he was concerned certain individuals brought him luck which others did not, Scindia in private life was a most loyal friend to all whom he liked and, if they were in trouble, he would cheerfully undergo any personal inconvenience to help or inspirit them. His regard for a man to whom he felt himself indebted did not die with the other's death. In various ways he would continually recall the memory of such an one. The nomenclature of the Shivpuri roads will remind posterity of many persons who in his youth had influenced Scindia for good or had otherwise engaged his affections.

For the poor or for those in misfortune he had a sympathy that was as practical as it was genuine. From his private purse unostentatiously he would time and again help some victim of hard luck and set him on his feet once more. Such aid he would extend to people regardless of their race or creed. He was often imposed on, but a recognition of the fact did not make him less generous on another occasion. To-day all over India there are prominent business men who owe their start or success in life or their rescue from financial disaster to the ungrudging help in money or in personal influence given them by the late Maharaja. There are also to be found many of Eastern or Western parentage who traded on his open-hearted liberality for their private ends, and considered it no shame to cheat him who had assisted them and who possibly had given them well paid employment when they were in desperate straits. In such cases it was never the loss of his money that affected Scindia; rather it was the bitter realisation of such disloyalty to a friend that caused him deep mental distress.

No saint himself, he expected no high standard of morality either from the world at large or from those who fell under the charm of his personality. It was characteristic of his nature to make no serious effort to draw a veil over his private failings in order to make his life in public appear spotless. He had none of the aloofness and cloistered futility that such a position as his so often induces. Ever in the public eye, he had no wish to hide from it his spontaneous impulses or the actions to which those impulses led, actions which the more sophisticated and less self-confident would carefully reserve for the narrowest circle of their intimate friends. He not only held that Humanity everywhere is subject to the same affections and appetites but that all the world must yield to those feelings, the only difference between men being that, while some posed as conquerors of Nature, others frankly recognised her superiority. This belief engendered in him a hard practicability which in its decisiveness was often disconcerting and always amazing.

The only sin for which he could imagine no forgiveness was the crime of disloyalty. A man who had not been true to his salt could never hope to regain the confidence of Scindia. He was far more likely to be pursued with real vindictiveness, for Scindia, who was usually a big man and sometimes a great man, was in certain respects always painfully small. In his intensely human temperament all the noble qualities were deeply tinctured with their neighbouring extravagances. There is nothing surprising in this, for as has been well said:—"A man's temperament is all the man. Men juggle with temperament as they do with words, phrases, theories, whims, and fads; and it rarely occurs to people who reason from a sentimental stand-point to analyse their feelings. Stamp with a seal of sincerity any preposterous theory, and there will not be wanting sentimental people to accept it."

Possibly many of Scindia's greatest successes were due to the fact that his personality time and again was by its very extravagances able to turn the hard-headed into sentimentalists.

With Europeans in every grade of society Scindia's relations were, as a rule, most cordial; though, towards the end of his life, thanks to the ill-manners of some who were bound to honour him, the ingratitude of others who had every reason to reverence him as their benefactor, and the dishonesty of a few who were a disgrace to their country, he lost faith and became distrustful in the case of any new acquaintances who sought his patronage or association with him in business. Nevertheless he remained staunch towards his old and tried friends for whom his affection never abated. With age too his respect for well-bred Englishmen and the scions of aristocratic families visibly increased. He had been unfortunate in his intercourse with Europeans at the period of his greatest social and administrative activity; but the only result of this was to make him more discriminating in his choice of friends. And yet the origin of the genuine friendships he formed with many Englishmen was not his position, for often he would conceal the fact that he was a Ruling Prince: it was his complete freedom from all pride and affectation rather that first attracted strangers. In England, for instance, he would derive the keenest pleasure from seeing one of his gorgeously liveried menials mistaken for the Maharaja of Gwalior while, chuckling, he stood in the background.

In the obituary notice published by a certain London newspaper appears a story which Scindia more than once told of himself. The occasion was one of the many festivities connected with the Coronation of of His Majesty King Edward VII. On a particular evening, having no official engagement, the Maharaja went unattended into the City to see the illuminations. He soon lost his way and asked his whereabouts from a passer-by. The individual addressed took pity on "the poor Indian whose untutored mind" he correctly assumed to be innocent of the topography of London. A member of the working classes, he had brought out his wife and the baby to look at the illuminations. In a happy mood, he was over-flowing with good will. "Stick to me, Tommy," he said. "I'll keep yer from 'arm."

They went along and gazed at the spectacle. Trust begot trust, and soon Scindia was taking his share in carrying the baby. A very good baby it was (we have his word for it) it did not cry once. Presently, tired of the sight, Scindia proposed to give his chance-met acquaintances some supper. The invitation was accepted after some hesitation once the workman and his wife had been assured that the expense would not be too much for their companion's pocket. The simple folk were much impressed by the comparative grandeur of the restaurant whither they were conducted. It was useless to offer them champagne; they preferred the beer of which Scindia too partook. The size of the tip to the waiter astonished them. They insisted that their host must be a very wealthy man and were obviously less at their ease than before. Scindia, however, restored their comfort by insisting that he too was a working man, though his master paid him well for service in his stables!

As they parted at the restaurant door and Scindia bade good-bye to his guests, not forgetting the baby, who, as its mother remarked, had taken "a real liking" to him, the workman blurted out the words:

"Well, Tommy, yer ain't exactly our sort of course, but yer *are* a damned good chap."

As the anonymous author of the obituary notice rightly observes, it was a just criticism. For all his achievements as a Ruler, Madhav Rao Scindia would have preferred remembrance for his personal qualities. If the writers of these words may gauge his wish in the matter, he would have liked above everything to go down to posterity as what he was, as "a damned good chap."

CHAPTER XII.

THE FUTURE?

THE preceding pages have attempted a sketch of Madhav Rao Scindia's life and work as two persons saw and see them. In places the drawing may be faulty and the colours here too bright, there too dull; but, even on the presumption that the picture as a whole is no utter failure, its painters have no right to arrogate to themselves the functions of a college of prophets. Any estimate of what the future holds in store for Gwalior should be a problem for grave political philosophers, not the subject for wild vaticinations by amateurs in letters. Prediction therefore will be eschewed.

Less out of place, perhaps, may be a brief statement of the difficulties confronting those persons to whom the late Maharaja has entrusted the conduct of State affairs during the minority of his only son; less out of place, since those very difficulties are largely a legacy from the peculiar successes of Scindia as a Ruler.

If, during his life-time, His Highness set his senior officials many a stiff piece of work, he never gave them a task half so perplexing as that which he has bequeathed them at his death. His servants—for they still regard themselves as such—have to carry on the administration of Gwalior as far as possible along the lines he has laid down for them. At first glance things appear ridiculously simple. The Majlis-i-Khas or State Executive Council has automatically become the Council of Administration with the Senior Maharani Sahiba as its President.

But there is a speciousness about this apparent simplicity. The rule of the dead Chief was so informed by his own innate genius that no Council, however able, can hope to possess a fraction of the prestige that enabled "Madho Maharaj" to secure such striking results in every branch of his administration. In his view, for there to be any virtue in personal rule, the rule had to be personal, and his government was a success just, indeed only, because it was so. His political trustees have to do the best they can, deprived of his personality. It is not that they have to make bricks without straw, for at their disposal they have practically all the material resources on which he could draw. It is rather as if they had not the stamp with which to impress on the bricks in their making that special mark for which the good people of Gwalior are wont to look so as to assure themselves that those bricks are of those same excellent quality as that to which their lost leader accustomed them.

It must be conceded that, at the date of his investiture with ruling powers, Madhav Rao Scindia admirably suited the times and conditions as he then found them in Gwalior. Conditions altered, the times moved on, but his versatile brain was fully able to cope with changes for which it was to a great measure responsible. Assuming that Gwalior had remained an autocracy, it is an interesting, if a vain, problem to estimate for how long, had his life been spared, his administrative ability, backed by all the prestige he had so deservedly won, would have continued competent to deal with the ever accelerating rate of social and political progress in his State. With the same assumption as above, it is a problem of practical importance to conjecture the length of time for which any Council can guide that progress wisely and not just mark time. It appears a problem of practical importance, but it is too difficult a riddle for solution by the joint authors of this memoir.

There is no question of the introduction of a bureaucratic, still less of a popular, form of government into the State. Gwalior to-day has been left an autocracy, and it is the bounden duty of the Council to hand it over as such to the young Maharaja to do what he likes with it, once he assumes control. Yet, at the moment, British India is pursuing the will-o-the-wisp of democracy, that political phantom after which Western Civilization has been blindly chasing. The sentiment of tradition and the lack of imagination, inherent in bureaucracy, that stolid counterpoise to democracy, may save Mother India from disaster. If she gets bogged in the mire, stolid permanent officials may pull her out, before she has sunk too deep. But, in Gwalior, if any Jack-o'-lantern allures the ignorant into some political swamp, rescue work will be no easy matter.

From all sides false prophets may come, thinking the State a fertile soil for the propagation of the damnable heresy that in heads numbers count more than brains and that the majority is always right. Mischief-makers too may try to resurrect in Gwalior the hideous spectre of communal strife that for years was laid by Madhav Rao Scindia's powerful charm, by his curse on all religious bigotry. Or, again, a venomous section of the British Indian Press, now that the champion of Gwalior is no more, may dare to raise its head and hiss at that child of His Highness's own brain, his pet scheme of a minority administration, which the Supreme Government is genuinely anxious to foster.

While his people remember their dead Ruler as the man he really was, that is before he becomes a golden myth, the plots of the evilly disposed should meet with little encouragement. But too often in India a great man soon after his passing is illumined by a blaze of sentimental light which blinds his worshippers to those very features that should most evoke their reasoned and lasting admiration.

That the Council of Administration must eschew individualism and concentrate on "team work" is as obvious to its members as to their critics. That parochial politics can have no place in their actions or deliberations is a platitude which they find at least as stale as the rest of the world. Yet, assuming that the dangers of individual or parochial predilection are avoided, as they must be, the difficulties that remain are still stupendous.

In modern times no government, no autocracy least of all, can afford to stand still. The advance of civilisation necessitates continual adjustments in any administrative machine, if it is to function properly. Madhav Rao Scindia would have been the last to affirm that the mechanism which he left at his death was fool-proof, still less that it was perfect in its design. To the end he was always experimenting with it, indeed sometimes tinkering at parts of it unnecessarily.

For the common weal of those subjects whom he loved, adjustments will constantly have to be made; but will those affected by the necessary changes be found ready to admit the efficacy of the hands which now regulate those adjustments? Much will depend not only on the wisdom but on the tact with which the alterations are made, for no trustees can hope for a tithe of the prestige earned by him who nominated them for their position of trust. In reforms which are the work of an individual, the world may recognise ideal motives; in those, made by a collective body, no aim save that of utility is ever admitted by ubiquitous critics.

The Gwalior Council is doubtless aware that History records no instance of any minority administration, however beneficent, attaining to even momentary popularity. The Councillors, then, will not vainly strive after applause. Such applause they will deserve, though they will not receive it, if they can preserve undimmed the brightest features of the administration of "Madho Maharaj."

Perhaps their fairest hope for the future lies in a clear recognition of what more than anything else made the rule of the late Maharaja so real a success. As a despot, he saw in his position no cause to seek for an expansion of his prerogatives; in it he searched only for wider opportunities for service. In the microcosm of Gwalior "Service" was as much his motto as it is that of Henry Ford in the industrial world. That is one thing which the Council can do; it can give service. Individually or collectively, in or out of office hours, its members can be as accessible to any who need their help as was His Highness himself, while still alive. They can listen to the views of all sorts and conditions of men just as he did.

To take a metaphor from Irrigation, that branch of Civil Engineering in which the late Maharaja was most keenly interested, the life-work of Madhav Rao Scindia may be compared to the construction of a large dam which at his death he left unfinished. The design of the dam shows genius, not merely skill; its proposed dimensions are colossal; its base appears to be set on the solid rock. Certain sections of the structure have already risen to considerable heights, in other places the foundations have only just been put in. If the all-round level of construction had been more regular than it is, the total amount of masonry work so far completed would not have looked nearly so immense nor so impressive as it does to-day. Yet, to hold up any large quantity of water in the dam, the gaps between the high portions must now be filled in and filled in as quickly as good work allows.

The fitting of new ashlars between, those already in position is no easy problem even for experts, though an amateur world may not recognise the difficulty. Further, there is always a fear lest, while the work is at a critical stage, some wild spate may come and not only damage the new half-set masonry, but may even undermine the old foundations already in existence.

Still, whatever the dangers, in the course of the next few years, the gaps must be closed somehow and the whole wall raised to a uniform level on which George Jivaji Rao Scindia may build afresh or may place the coping stones. It is his dam to deal with as he likes, in any case.

Much will depend on the young Maharaja's natural abilities; much on his training for the job of political engineer. He may be content just to lay the coping stones, but, as his father's son, he is likely to want to raise the dam. In the latter event, he may recognise that, if the wall is to soar above the height already designed for it, its upstream face will need careful treatment with the cement of constitutionalism, for, with the political weather so uncertain, none can say how turbulent a flood the dam may be forced to withstand in the uncertain days which lie ahead of Gwalior.

FINIS.